♦ ♦ Heinke Pauly was born in Hamburg but ran away from home the day after she left school to live in sin with an Englishman in Moss Side, Manchester. They moved via Lewis in the Hebrides to a remote Orcadian island, where the native sheep eat seaweed and can swim. After almost ten years, she left those romantic shores, and went to study in Edinburgh. It was known at the time as Europe's 'Capital of AIDS' and she wrote a film-script addressing the issue of HIV+ women, as well as a few short stories. Once her three children had become independent survivors, she went for a short trip to Spain, only to end up living there. Enthusiastic hillwalker and choir singer, she is currently learning the art of sailing.

www.campingwithwolves.blogspot.com

The right of Heinke Pauly to be identified as the Author of this Work has been asserted by her in accordance with the Copyright, Designs and Patents Act 1998.

Copyright © Heinke Pauly 2009

All rights reserved. No part of this publication may be reproduced, stored in a retrieval system, or transmitted, in any form or by any means without the prior written permission of the publisher, nor be otherwise circulated in any form of binding or cover other than that in which it is published and without a similar condition being imposed on the subsequent purchaser. Any person who does so may be liable to criminal prosecution and civil claims for damages.

ISBN: 978-1-905988-67-9

'Extracts from 'As I Walked Out One Midsummer Morning' by Laurie Lee and 'Don Quixote' by Miguel de Cervantes Saavedra reproduced by permission of Penguin Books Ltd.

Published by Libros International

Printed and bound in Great Britain by
CPI Antony Rowe, Chippenham and Eastbourne

Camping with Wolves

Heinke Pauly

To Anne,
yes - it's all true!
love, Heinke.

Libros
International

Without the systematic electronic mastery ministered by Christina Fraser this story would probably have never got off the ground; without the weighed-up and kind encouragement of Nik Morton the story would have stayed in the cupboard; without the dog Misty Blue I might not have had the nerve to travel alone; and without the kind permission of Penguin engineered by Mary Fox to quote some words by Laurie Lee this project would have died at its conception.

For my grandson Peter, and Bob Dylan

Introduction

It was all Eleanor's fault. She - my distant neighbour in a Scottish village who first gave me the book that compelled me to camp my way through Spain. Her eyes twinkled as she handed me her old copy of Laurie Lee's 'As I Walked Out One Midsummer Morning' complete with hand-drawn map on the very first page. I was instantly hooked by the tale of a young man walking through Spain for a year and a half. Little did I know at the time that just over a year later I would have many a story to tell her after travelling, alone, through Spain.

Having lived in a Spanish tourist town for just over a year, I woke up early one morning realizing that I urgently needed some money. I let out my flat and soon found myself in the limestone canyons somewhere near Lorca, when an idea struck me.

Laurie Lee had walked from Vigo to Almuñecar, stopping here and there, for eighteen months, before being boatlifted back to Britain having witnessed the Spanish Civil War break out the very night before. My idea now tells meis to go to Almuñecar and relive the poet's journey exactly seventy years later. I have an old car, a cheap tent and my faithful blue merle border collie to help me make the journey backwards, south to north, living mainly on tomatoestomatoes and sardines, an ascetic diet similar to Laurie Lee's.

And I have one month.

Suddenly, I imagine myself climbing a mountain like a repentant sinner. I take one step, bend the knees, lie prostrate, stand and straighten, take another step, bend, lie prostrate...but that would just get me a load of odd looks as I'm testing my courage to see if I really have the guts to go it alone. Laurie was nineteen, but I am fifty-three. Also, a fifty pence-sized mushroom has erupted on my face, and the rent has not come in. This means I don't have money for petrol to go to Almuñecar just yet and I will have to wait for *mañana* in the mountains.

I have often wondered why Spain doesn't throw all its clocks away. The concept of Spanish time is so totally alien from mine, and time after time I'm struggling with more lessons in '*paciencia*'. Patience is a virtue, but I'm no saint. In fact, I am riddled with fear and anticipation. Is this really a test of courage or a totally foolish notion to travel without a planned destination, without roadside assistance in case the car breaks down, without money? True, I'm scared, dreading it really, the stress of it all growing a large blemish on my face, near my mouth. Is there maybe something I cannot express, and the blemish is its symbol?

I decide to stay with a friend to bide my time.

On the way to her place, road signs for Almería beckon in Arabic, but I leave the heavy traffic and turn off towards Caravaca, my face in flames, the mushroom steadily growing into a small tortoise.

30 April 2006

Sunday morning sees me waking up in a small house surrounded by mountains. I have no idea where I am. Then it all comes back to me: a large lady, Mercedes, climbing over the bar to welcome me to her restaurant, kissing my right and left cheek.

'Oh, careful,' I say, 'I think my tortoise is highly infectious!' She dismisses the lookalike animal on my chin with a flick of the wrist '*¡Nada!*' and brings us jugs of chilled sangria. The effect is almost instantaneous after the hot day and, as if intoxicated with a magic potion, I suddenly realize that I am fluent in Spanish as I tell Mercedes about my planned journey.

'*Pero estoy muy embarazada de mi cara,*' I remember saying. She looks at me sideways obviously considering my general mental health.

'*¿Embarazada?*' she asks, making the international sign for 'I'm going to have a baby', outlining a big egg-shaped curve in front of her abdomen. The tortoise and the rest of my face go bright red as I get the message. I had told her, 'But I am very pregnant of my face,' when I had meant to say 'embarrassed'. Then everybody else got it, and I felt like falling through an invisible door in the floor.

After a few sardines on toast, my friend and I climb the small hill with a huge white concrete Jesus towering above the little town of Archivel. We decide to go to Nerpio for the afternoon. She drives her Golf like a teenager on drugs. She hacks around hairpins and shoots along any straight bits in the narrow mountain road as if getting ready for take-off. I grip my seat in terror and hope my lunch (tomato) and breakfast combined will stay with me. Forever faking a supercool exterior, I check my lipstick in the wing mirror and go for some more.

Nerpio has a river running right through the centre with little waterfalls splashing everywhere and I immediately need to find a toilet. Over the cobbled bridge and into a bar by the river we are just sitting down for a *café con leche* when explosions go off in the near distance echoing around the old buildings. Misty, the dog, freaks and almost pulls the chair she is tied to, as well as me sitting on it, into the river to get away from the noise. Then we see the procession coming over the bridge, led by the most awful brass band playing 'New York, New York'. I feel the late onset of a hangover slowly trying to creep over me and identify a smoking moment. It is that time for a cigarette. More bangers go off and I hope the dog's head is not going to explode.

We race back, my friend praising her radials, past ancient caves carved into craggy rocks and across dried-up plains. Back at her ranch, which is a converted chicken farm, we hurriedly eat our short fast meal and my friend is off to watch a soap on TV.

Outside, a cigarette is calling for me as I wander along

straight new pavements lining the rows of ex-chicken houses. The neatly-kept terraced cottages, gaily-coloured with inviting doors, sit peacefully amongst the hills. I sit on a large rock, smoking. Still no money but, of course, it is the weekend. There will be money on Monday. Then it has to be processed. What exactly is that? Somebody somewhere typing lots of numbers into a computer and then click-send it to me? No, it is the mysterious process of processing. This can take days. A week even. I have another smoke to avoid screaming, ripping my hair out and smashing my skull against the rock.

On my way back, the pub is shut. I feel like I'm in detox surrounded by overflowing hanging baskets as if straight from a Miracle Gro advertisement. Laurie, where are you? The tortoise feels crumbly and is falling off my chin in hard dark scales, but it has grown a pregnant mass near my mouth. The cracks forming between the itchy ever-erupting scales hurt when I speak or eat. This morning's sardines on toast were crunched gingerly, grimacing oddly, and the large luncheon tomato was more sucked than bitten like an apple. I just could not get my mouth open. I would have preferred to eat the fantastically fragrant, bright red gazpacho soup for dinner with a teaspoon but I didn't want to look a complete wimp. Thankfully, smoking still works.

1 May 2006

Hurray! 1st of May!

And this one is a Monday. I decide to brutally shave two euros off my twenty-euro budget for the week after stealing some of Dee's (my enduring friend who has put me up all these days) Nivea moisturizer, to slap onto the tortoise. Ah, what cooling relief. Dear reader, this scaly unknown animal crawling across my face gives me no rest from itching, pain and burning again along raw open cracks. It is time for a treat. The *farmacia* does not stock the face cream. The *ferretería*'s frying pans are extortionate. The miniscule supermarket has thin tin pans ideal for cooking on camping gas. Oh no, the hand is reaching out, the other goes to touch the tortoise cheek. The head turns momentarily. I glimpse two jars of Nivea moisturizer on a different shelf. I take them both, the cream now in one hand and the pan in the other.

I have blown over a third of my weekly budget and trot back to the ranch through Archivel. Its one hole-in-the-wall tells me I have no money. It remains unprocessed. Ha! Misty has found a muddy puddle and is standing in it. Great. I just hope that her white paws covered in foul mud will have dried off by the time we get back. The dog loves Dee's rug, all fluffy white and beige and brown sheepskins sewn into a weave pattern. She makes straight for it but I catch her just in time to avoid disaster.

After breakfast, yes, more sardines on toast, Dee and I are off to the highest village in the Murcia region. We reckon it is called Los Odres. A mountain of the same name in the Revolcadores range next door is 1,880 metres above sea level. I can't figure out from the map if it is part of the Sierra Taibilla - yesterday's wild drive - or the Sierra Mojantes. And somehow, it doesn't matter.

We arrive at the end of the track and leave the car. There are maybe a dozen ramshackle houses, a new-looking restaurant and a riding school. There is nobody about as it is high noon and the Spanish people have taken to the shade. A sleepy, hot dog tries to follow us up the *cañada* but Misty sees him off immediately. The *cañadas* are cattle paths used by shepherds to drive animals from old pasture to new. It is said that the Visigoths started the practice of moving their animal herds south from Castilla Leon to Extremadura for the winter, avoiding the cold weather of winter in the north as well as giving the fields a chance to recuperate. In the Middle Ages, sheep became Spain's economic mainstay, and twice a year, during the '*trashumancia*' (migration of flocks and herds), enormous dust clouds would rise in the air above the large herds of animals. Some of these drove roads were up to seventy-five metres wide. Today, sheep are transported by trucks or trains, and many *cañadas* have been rendered useless due to new roads, growing cities or rubbish dumps. Yet there is a campaign to keep these historic 'drove' roads open (*Projecto 2001*), and every year, on Midsummer's Day, a flock of around two thousand sheep is taken through downtown Madrid, not just to keep up a tradition but also to stop the loss of public land and for obvious environmental reasons.

We only climb a short distance and decide it's far too hot to be walking. So out comes the picnic lunch: sardines, tomatoes, a hunk of crunchy fresh white bread, an orange for Dee, and water. I wish I had not forgotten the binoculars. There are some huge raptors circling above a mountaintop and I am dying to know if they might be eagles. Ah well.

On the way back we talk of Cervantes. I imagine Don Quixote charging into two dust clouds he has spotted in the distance, thinking they are armies of valiant knights about to do battle, when in fact they are just a huge pile of sheep trotting along some *cañada*. I had stopped reading 'Don Quixote' altogether because the tale of the beautiful shepherdess annoyed me terribly. It was not just the style of writing, undoubtedly fashionable at the time, with lots of long-winded, embroidered descriptions and explanations, hardly any paragraphs and the tiny print of my cheapo edition. No, it was the attitude of the goatherds in the story that got to me. Or had I fallen directly into the trap carefully set by Cervantes? After all, did he not write 'Don Quixote' as a very tongue-in-cheek response to the social climate of the time, filled with stories about 'valiant knights' whose kitsch morals had got up his nose? What happened in the story about the beautiful shepherdess is this. Don Quixote and Sancho spend some nights camping with a group of goatherds. Sancho would have preferred otherwise but Don Quixote reckons sleeping under the stars, out in the open, will confirm 'his title to knighthood by a new act of possession'. Does he mean 'experience'? They argue a bit on their first night. After a dinner of dried acorns and cheese 'as hard as a brick' with plenty of 'skins' (wine skins) offered by the goatherds, Sancho wants the singing and music to stop so he can go to sleep. At this, Don Quixote teases him mercilessly about the amount of wine he has drunk, enough to induce sleep at his estimation despite the continuous 'finest' singing.

Then a young man arrives with the news that the 'fine shepherd and scholar Chrysostom died this morning, ... and they say it was for love of that devilish untoward lass Marcella, rich William's daughter, that goes up and down the country in the habit of a shepherdess'. In his will, Chrysostom stated that he wanted to be buried at the foot of a mountain where he had first met Marcella. The whole village was in uproar as the ceremony was believed to be quite pagan. The scholar had advised farmers what to plant successfully through his use of astrology and everybody admired him. Not so Marcella. After her parents died, she was raised by her uncle, who was a parson. She grew more beautiful by the day and had suitors calling on her uncle for her hand from all over the country. But she felt too young to 'burden' herself with wedlock, and in the end got fed up with the hordes of enraptured men, so she took off to the mountains to become a shepherdess. She would talk with men who were well behaved yet, as soon as love and adoration were mentioned, she would cast them out. And why not? Because she was so beautiful and men fell in love with her left, right and centre did not mean that she was obliged to yield to their advances. This made her a proud and cold heartbreaker in the men's opinion. At the funeral, Chrysostom's friends were musing on his poem

'The Despairing Lover', when Marcella herself appeared at the top of the mountain. She said that she had never encouraged the young man nor flirted with him, quite the contrary. 'He persisted, though I had given him a due caution, and he despaired without being hated. Now I leave you to judge, whether I ought to be blamed for his sufferings? If I have deceived, let him complain; if I have broke my promise to anyone, let him despair; if I encourage anyone, let him presume; if I entertain anyone, let him boast: but let no man call me cruel nor murderer, until I either deceive, break my promise, encourage or entertain him. Heaven has not been pleased to show whether it is its will I should love by destiny, and it is vain to think I will ever do it by choice: so let this general caution serve every one of those who make their addresses to me for their own ends.' There's my girl, go get them told. She goes on for another page justifying herself, finishing with these words: 'My thoughts are limited by these mountains; and if they wander further, it is only to admire the beauty of Heaven, and thus, by steps, to raise my soul towards her original dwelling.' Then she runs off into the woods. Some of the awestruck men at the funeral ceremony immediately want to run after her, but Don Quixote steps in at once. 'Let no man,' cried he, 'of what quality or condition so ever, presume to follow the fair Marcella, under the penalty of incurring my furious displeasure. She has made it appear, by undeniable reason, that she was not guilty of Chrysostom's death; and has positively declared her firm resolution never to condescend to the desires of any of her admirers: for which reason, instead of being importuned and persecuted, she ought to be esteemed and honoured by all good men, as being perhaps the only woman in the world that ever lived with such virtuous reservedness.'

Once the grave was covered in a great stone, Chrysostom's best friend planned to have a monument made bearing an epitaph: 'Here of a wretched swain, The frozen body's laid, Kill'd by the cold disdain Of an ungrateful maid' etc, despite Don Quixote's words.

I had previously summed up this story as 'Young bloke declares his everlasting but she doesn't want to know and moves away to the mountains to be without men but live only with sheep. He dies of a broken heart and she gets the blame for it! As his friends dig his grave she turns up on the top of a rocky ledge explaining that the men's thoughts of resentment are not acceptable'. My friend wanted more detail so that we could really get our teeth into the subject of 'men'. No, we are not man-haters or spikey, blue-haired punks who generalize too much. We are ladies of a certain age, with attitude. I was so angry at the injustice of it all; I mean, here is a man positively obsessed with love to the point that his 'victim', the young girl, has to run off and live in the mountains! I put the book away, grumpy and vexed. Obviously off on a daily rant, I jabber on how Cervantes died on the same day (St George's) as Shakespeare as if that had anything to do with anything. But really, was Cervantes being ironic or trying to illuminate the dark spaces in our lives? Don Quixote was going to offer his services to Marcella once he found her but told the goatherds that he planned to clean the area of thieves and robbers instead. Had he also not really taken in Marcella's words? As it turned out, something happened to cross his plans. Cervantes, the sorcerer of words, promises a sequel 'of this true history' and then stops the book.

Suspense ending or what.

We stop the car, having arrived back at the house. Dee makes some lovely leek soup, but it makes me fart, so I am glad to sit outside after dinner on a posh swinging sofa at the back of the house, taking in the sunset. Looking through an ancient Beatles songbook, we sing some of them badly. I have a wee dram of whisky to open the throat. I am beginning to get scared that my drinking arm might rot off due to sheer lack of exercise. After several cigarette moments, smoking does go so well with drinking, we retire inside. I go for the keyboard on the floor, Dee gets the drums, and we're off into never-neverland singing Dusty's tunes. Then Dee shows me her belly dancing techniques and assorted pelvic wobbles. The dog is hiding under the bed. It must be time to sleep.

2 May 2006

The silent morning sees a fat fluffy sparrow waddling unfirmly from rooftile to rooftile. Mum is shouting as if a cat has appeared until Dad arrives with a worm. The chick is chirping plaintively as the neighbourhood slowly begins to stir.

Inside, the huge fridge is humming rhythmically in the corner, there is an occasional soft dripping sound from the bathroom, Dee's sleepy breathing, and the neighbours faffing around in their kitchen.

I wonder if the walls are laughing? From chicken shed to luxury two-bed cottage - these walls have seen some changes! Would there have been two hundred chickens per two-bed house, clucking egg tunes through their feathered necks, scratching with three-toed feet for lost seeds in the dirt, looking sideways, one eye only, a close-up at a potential morsel? Misty is still asleep on the fabulous furry rug covering polished marble, dreaming of sheep and mountain goats with bells around their necks.

Over tea and sardines on toast Dee tells me that we are going to Caravaca with her neighbours to see the horses.

The large TV is already spewing out unwanted news and I can hardly make out what my friend is saying. Horses?

Dee and the neighbours are wearing white tops and red scarves. In the car I learn that when the castle of Caravaca was under siege, the Knights Templar saved the day. The castle had finally run out of water so they raced into the castle - just like that; maybe it was siesta - and brought wine, thus ensuring the survival of the inhabitants.

Today the annual tradition of running with the 'wine horses' is being honoured. Everybody is wearing white and red, even babies in prams. The buzz in the town is incredible. There is a small market to buy silly hats or *churros* and hot chocolate or the usual tourist trash knick-knacks. Dee buys us all a silly hat, I buy tiger balm for the tortoise. People are lining the streets when suddenly a band starts up, and here is the first horse, dressed from head to toe in hand-embroidered precious material, depicting the history of the Knights Templar and this town. A white horse is ridden by a stunning princess who waves regally at the cheering crowds.

Altogether, it feels like a crazy rave-up, the horses being paraded in front of the screaming loud band, only to race like mad along the crowded street and back again to jubilant applause, whistling men, and the clapping of hundreds of hands. This has been going on since 6 a.m. with free beer and wine for the crowds around the castle, leaving many faces dazed-looking and glassy-eyed. We wander off to find four enormous pots boiling paella over open fires, and María who is in charge of feeding three hundred people. Usually, she works for Mercedes' restaurant, but today she is volunteering for the fiesta. She hands us plates of steaming paella, with extra meat.

We scan the English version of the tourist brochure, which is pretty long-winded. Skip this if you're not ready for it.

I'm giving it to you raw and undiluted. This is how it goes: '*Since 1998, Caravaca de La Cruz is one of five towns in the world where the 'Permanent Jubilee Year' is celebrated. The other towns are Rome, Jerusalem, Santiago de Compostela and Santo Toribio de Liebana. From 2003 onwards, this holy celebration will be held every seven years, and the pilgrims who visit Caravaca shall receive the plenary indulgence. The year of 1996 attracted 700,000 pilgrims to the town. The Holy See acknowledges the long history of devotion to the Vera Cruz which dates back eight centuries. In the XVI and XVII centuries, Franciscans, Jesuits and Carmelites of San Juan de La Cruz and Santa Teresa established convents here. Later, they extended their cults to the rest of Europe and Latin America. In 1981 and 1996, the celebrations of Jubilee Year were granted, for the first reasons of 750th anniversary of the Apparition of the Vera Cruz, and in pursuance of the tradition that commenced in the XII century. On the 3rd of May 1232, the Moor king Ceyt-Abuceyt and his subjects became Christians on seeing the miracle of the Apparition of Santa Cruz which was lowered from the heavens by two angels so that the priest Ginez Perez Chirinos, who was a prisoner in the fortress at the time, could say Mass. On contemplating this Apparition, the Moor king and all his court embraced the Christian Faith. The Catholic Church acknowledges it as the Vera Cruz, or True Cross, a title that was only used for the cross found by Santa Isabel, the mother of the Emperor Constantine. This cross was divided into three parts, and deposited in*

Jerusalem, Constantinople and Rome. Since then, the title of Vera Cruz has been used to distinguish the fake relics from the true ones. In 1736, it gained such importance that it was given the Cult of Latria, similar to the one received by the Holy Sacrament. The Vera Cruz in the silver chest donated by the Master Suarez de Figueroa is located in the church sanctuary. All of the inhabitants of the city and many pilgrims wear the image of the sacred relic around their necks, which is blessed during Mass of 1st of May.'

Ooof, so much history and it is not even mentioned in my guidebook.

It is only a small place with its twenty-four thousand residents, but it has a gorgeous medieval city centre, a beautiful church with an enormous stone scallop shell at the entrance, symbol of the pilgrims, and yes, there are crosses everywhere: in the shops, on walking sticks, wine labels, earrings, rings, teacups, lacy curtains, and even on the metal lids covering the road drains.

With the heat getting the better of us, we are soon all crossed out and head back to Archivel. Here we enter the cool shade of Mercedes' bar for refreshments. She generously hands us small dishes of olives, some with nuts. The little brown dishes should really be underneath plantpots in my opinion, but here in Spain they are called '*tapas*' (lids) and are used for serving a variety of treats. A tiny local man joins our table, telling me there is a healer woman living in the village who can make my tortoise disappear overnight. Perplexed, I tell him, 'Thank you, but I am a homeopath and can cure myself.'

Dee is digging her elbow into my ribs at this point, whispering, 'Don't trust him, he has dirty shoes'.

He explains that he has been drinking beer since 6 a.m.,

gratis, and been running with the wine horses. Dee's neighbour reckons it is time for the next round and tries to sell me to the stranger so we can get some more drinks in. I flee and take Misty for an evening walk amongst fields of young green wheat, shiny in the evening light.

3 May 2006

Wild tiger balm on cold sores stings with such a furious fire, I feel my face might explode off the front of my head. Desperately tired of being 'poxy-chops', I rub more of the cure-all balm into the burning cracks.

Slept badly last night, dreaming of someone who arrived with lots of fish, then would not go away. Next, I was saving everybody from a ship swaying between huge waves, across slimy bridges et cetera, only to find all the fish in the fridge had come alive - a blind monkfish opened its groaning jaws, eels wiggled and slid all over the fridge and out of it. Thankfully woke up because Misty jumped on me and I heard it then: the unmistakable plop-plop of fat raindrops falling onto roofs, tables and chairs. It is 2 a.m. and a thunderstorm is rolling over the mountains. I spring out of bed to rescue the dictionary left outside.

Back to sleep, I dream of the car being squished by an unknown source, forced neatly into a concertinaed shape between a hedge and another hedge. Then I'm back in Edinburgh, in the old tenement flat, but what's this? A lot of floors are not there, most inconvenient when you need to find your trousers and realize you're in bed with the wrong man.

In reality, I realiserealize this morning that I've forgotten Janis's survival coat, (another caring friend, a woman not the coat). It's the size of a small tent, warm and totally waterproof. Hmm, bad news. What to do if it rains like this for the camping, the day after tomorrow? The tent does not have a flysheet. Secretly I feel like going back to get the coat. It would be a long way back, just for a coat, but I hadn't considered so much rain. But who in their right mind starts a journey by going back?

Anyway, hurrah, today I have the money! Unbelievably, I feel like whooping it up right here in this small street where three out of the five cars don't drive but only park badly, where I've found a thin shallow frying pan, where I've walked and dreamt and hoped and now, here it is, cash, harsh cash: actually, pieces of paper, 'cash', numbers on paper, power, silver strips. Its ironed notes are singing songs of paper hopes, here in my unbelieving palm, to be folded into four neat pleats, fitting into the small zip of my purse, I am Croesus himself, the new goddess of finance. However, Mercedes has invited Dee and me to her place in Caravaca for tomorrow night, when the grand procession takes place. How could we refuse such a gesture of friendship.

Today, Dee and I are off to explore Calasparra. Here, in the middle of a nature reserve, is a big cave where a shepherd found a statue of the Holy Virgin in 1892. He tried to lift it but couldn't manage to move it. Later, a whole load of blokes also tried to shift the statue, without success. Of course, the cave was instantly declared holy. We see little effigies of haloed Holy Virgins in glass cupboards in the tourist trinket shop, but where is the real thing? In the cave's church, water is dripping through rock, then air, then onto more rock, plop-plop, like Joyce's image of the overflowing fountain, every drop sounding like the cricket bat hitting the ball. Plop, plop, plop.

Up some steps, behind the altar, a cavey room is filled with wedding dresses, baby clothes, christening gowns, and confirmation kits, all adorning the walls from ceiling to floor. Two men in sombre mood are hanging up more tiny suits and gowns using long sticks to reach the rails at the top.

Another room, similarly done up but with waxen babies' legs, heads, photos, green L- plates, chopped off ponytails attached to rails, paper prayers tied everywhere with red ribbons - 'thank you for getting me through that accident', 'please look after the health of my brothers and me', 'thank you for protecting my son's health I will remember you in all my prayers forever'. I am shattered with emotion as people walk by; how can they walk by, just like that, as I am filled with the pains of compassion, bereavement, sacrifice, and death. How can they be talking, sucking lollipops with just the stick protruding from their mouths, taking flash photos of the altar, and lighting little candles?

Back in the shop downstairs amongst the walking sticks, miniature statues in fake caves, key rings bearing crosses and other Catholic clutter, people are noisy, busy buying rosaries. MoreOutside, more people continue to arrive by the coachload throughout the grey day.

We take the dog for a walk by the river through dripping forest and bleached wet fields. After looking in on some of Dee's friends who live in the area, we are our return journey back through drizzly rain. Dee has a surprise lined up for me: dinner at Mercedes' bar.

For starters, we feast on salad with everything beautiful, tomatoes, olives, asparagus, boiled eggs, fresh lettuce, cucumber, followed by a huge platter of roast lamb cooked over the open fire in the restaurant, with chips. Dee must have her chips or she is not a happy bunny. For '*postres*' (dessert) I choose the pale yellow wobbly stuff in a *tapas* dish. It tastes like crème caramel with cinnamon on the top and fresh cream. There's also wine and *café con leche*. What a treat! Thanks, Dee.

4 May 2006

Clumps of wild poppies are splattered like blasts of arterial-red blood through the fields of corn swaying gently in the wind. The sky is still grey. Today is market day. There are only three stands at the market, two with flowers, one with vegetables and fruit. A far cry from the market in the place I have left behind. Its market is the biggest in the entire region of Valencia. I buy some lovely tomatoes and think of the evening to come. Tonight is the night.

By 7 p.m. we are decked out in party gear and take off to Caravaca. The streets are lined with metal football terraces, already filling up with cheerful crowds. Everybody and their grandparents keep arriving in a continuous throng. The spectators have brought long sticks of bread, drinks in cans, wine. Some have even brought entire smoked pigs' legs, *jamón serrano*, and tied them to the railings, deftly slicing fine slivers of the delicate meat for everyone around. Bangers rip through the air and go off, exploding with loud cracks on the pavements.

We're shoving and pushing our way to reach Mercedes'

flat. She welcomes us with great ceremony which means a vast amount of introductions and cheek-kissing goes on.

'This is my neighbour,' kiss, kiss, 'this is my best friend from my schooldays, she has come from Madrid,' kiss, kiss, et cetera. Her husband introduces me to three nice-looking guys perched on the balcony.

'They are all priests,' says the husband, grinning at me from ear to ear. No kiss, kiss. Instead, shared cigarettes and Spanish explanations of what is happening *en la calle*, in the street.

'It is the procession celebrating the Moors' and the Christians' traditions, their dress, music, dances.' The tall priest is superfriendly and offers more cigarettes and wine. He tells me that it takes the entire year to prepare for the procession and, when the young participants are selected, fights frequently break out because everybody wants to be in the Moors groups, not the Christians. I can see why. Here they come now, dancing girls in flowing gowns, skirts split into flapping trousers tied at the ankles, exposing bellies adorned with bejewelled belts, tinkling bells ding from their delicately moving hands.

The priests lean over the balcony in unison to check out the girly talent more closely.

Thirty or more gorgeous dancing girls are followed by the band, dressed in soft boots, Turkish-looking trousers, long hooded capes and turbans adorned with star and sickle moon, playing outlandish curling tunes to brilliant rhythms and energetic drumming. Now, the girls turn as one from right to left like a gigantic multi-coloured butterfly. The crowd gasps, then there are waves of applause, stamping of hundreds of feet. Here are a prince and princess on fiery horses, bedecked in embroidered blankets, prancing from side to side. Children reach out to touch the princess's scarf for good luck. More applause.

This goes on for two hours; different dancers, different bands. Suddenly a more serious tone overcomes the atmosphere as the stomping Christians' arrival is announced by a vast drum beating bombastically like a clock striking beyond midnight. Men in heavy leather boots tramp along carrying swords slashing at the night air like a fierce enemy. The girls arrive wearing chaste dresses and medieval, tall, pointy hats with thin veils attached or flat ribbons tying their hair into nets. Their dances are set to a square dance routine and remind me of Scottish country dancing. The bands make oompah oompah noises reminiscent of Bavarian beer tents. I can see why fights break out. The Moors are far more flamboyant.

But a priest beckons from the dining room; the food is ready. The large table is groaning under the weight of the feast laid out. There is everything and more. *Jamón*, olives, cheeses, bread, *tortilla*, *paella*, all sorts of vegetables and fruits, little meatballs, a special stew cooked by María, little *boquerones*, fish baked in bechamel and nutmeg sauce, wine and more wine. Waves of more applause waft through the open windows as we are munching on the delicacies. Mercedes' husband jokes at one of the priests, 'You might have given the blessing' or something I don't quite understand, but the guy goes bright red and immediately puts his plate on the table to thank the Lord for the food.

Costumes and '*costumbres*', customs.

After another two hours of procession, Dee and I make

our excuses and exit. Little did I know that she cannot see in the dark and was terrified to drive back through the black night.

5 May 2006

Hurrah, I'm on the road! I even managed to rescue my mascot from Dee: the small plastic giraffe! I found it on a sandy beach after having climbed over a six-foot wire mesh fence when, just at the top and about to turn over or fall off, my phone rang. Of course, I couldn't take the call, from some finished relationship - I had to hang on - cling onto the fence, hold on for dear life itself. When I finally jumped down onto the sandy beach, I saw it. A small plastic giraffe the size of half of my hand was lying in the sand, looking at me. I picked it up and carried it around in my rucksack like a mascot, symbolizing that all fences can be overcome despite old boyfriends, and obstacles can be turned into opportunities.

Desperate for distance, solitude maybe, the freedom of the road, my red car slices through sheets of pelting rain like a hot knife through butter. Up and up goes the winding road, and bit by bit the rain abates.

In Pliego I stock up on tomatoes, bread and sardines. I leave town with some difficulty as I cannot find any road signs on the small C3315 to lead me in the right direction. After having gone in a circle twice, I ask a small, bewildered-looking man whom I have passed twice. I should have trusted my instinct. The man tells me I was quite right to take some small road leading further up into the mountains. Once the rain has stopped, I pull into a forest track and put the kettle on. You see, when I have tea shortage, I lose the plot a bit. Luncheon consists of two sardine sandwiches, then it's back on the road.

Eventually, I reach my destination: the campsite at El Berro in the Sierra Espuna. A fat raincloud has gone over but not a drop has fallen. I am surrounded by limestone mountains covered in pine forests. Somewhere a cockerel crows- announcing my arrival? Birds have started to sing and chat. Good grief, there's a car! The first I have seen for what seems like hours. The yellow gorse sends wafts of coconut perfume into the grey air.

Misty goes berserk at the campsite warden, barking ferociously and baring frightening fangs from the back of the car. Dogs are allowed on the site but have to be kept on a lead. The tent is up within minutes, but Misty is in a bad mood due to her extended lead made from the washing line. Resigned to sitting next to her water bowl, she is throwing me sullen looks as I set up the kitchen in the back of the car. Over several cups of tea, taken in the fab folding plastic chair, I survey the scene. There are a number of stationary caravans but only two other people on the entire site. The peace is exquisite.

Misty and I take a walk past a cemetery and up to the top of the small hill behind the village. I sit down under the white concrete statue of Jesus, overlooking the entire plains, backed by the mountains of the sierra. There it is, that cigarette moment. Church bells are echoing around the small houses and huge mountains, calling evening Mass. Feeling on top of the world, Misty and I run

around a bit, me throwing and her catching sticks.
Then I see it.

At first it looks like a long stick but within seconds it has reared its head. Something screams inside me, 'Help, a long grey snake,' but the thing is already slithering off into the undergrowth. My blood pressure has nearly given me a stroke or some sort of seizure. The pure shock of it. The last time I saw a snake was in a zoo. Terror-struck, I decide on the spot that I better get used to MMother Nature'sother Nature's surprises at once. Shaking and trembling, II immediately have anotheranother cigarette to steady the nerves and calm myself down. Once more restored to my former self, I pick some wild thyme to sprinkle over the planned dinner of sliced tomato and cucumber with some fresh, chopped garlic. This might not make me smell that good, but I hope it will keep the mosquitoes away. I resolve to be really careful walking about freestyle, in case of more apparent 'grey sticks' suddenly rear their heads.

Back on site, the dog back on the lead, Friday night mayhem has broken out. People are everywhere, cars and vans driving around the place trying to find their allocated space. Although dusk is setting in, most of them are wearing shades, talking incessantly, putting up their tents. Some cyclists are racing uphill behind me; campervans arrive and get stuck in the bends of the track; and kids are running, kicking a ball. It's after 9 p.m. and the two guys opposite me are still pumping something up. How this can take over half an hour, I don't know. They have a couple of dismantled bicycles upside down, ready to get the wheels back on.

I hope the rain will hold off. Final toilet trip, and soon the falling darkness will forgive all.

6 May 2006

At 6 a.m. all hell breaks loose. Zips screech, radio alarm clocks go off, phones ring, doors bang, people shout, cars start revving up. Last night's mystery is explained - the guys were pumping up tyres for their bikes to go for some 'Raid World Race' practice, perhaps a bit like cross-country cycling, I guess.

Suddenly, it's all over and the dawn chorus resumes its birdy tunes. Oh, no. Here we go again. A bundle of blokes in Lycra are butchly running uphill with lots of ropes the length of the campsite. I reckon they must be some crazy abseilers. Help - I've landed in some outdoor activity centre, and now they're all out and active except for my pensioner neighbours next door, unless they both died during the night. It was pretty cold. I have several hot cups of tea and a tin of sardines spread on leftover bread.

The tortoise is still creeping its scaly brown patch across my face. I look scary. In the hope that people will not point at me and women gather their children as I walk by bearing my marks of leprosy, I shyly venture forth into the village. In the one shop, Manu Chao is playing in the background. I immediately chill out and get talking with the *señora* who runs the place, wearing a snow-white lace-edged apron. The tomatoes come on Mondays, '*tardes*', late afternoon, '*claro*'; how many miles must a tomato travel before it is sold. Meat comes on Thursdays, but she has an enormous fridge, immaculately clean, with some fresh sausages.

'White or red? Or two of each?'

'*Sí, muy bien.*'

She tells me the music is from the local radio station; the campsite gets quite busy in the summer; there are two bakeries, '*panaderías*', over here and over there, and two small *restaurantes* selling roast chickens.

A round dumpling *señora* walks in. It's '*Buenos días*' all round, and she joins the conversation. 'Mass is at 6 a.m., 12 noon, then 7.30 p.m.. Those are very good sausages you are buying. I have only come in for my chocolate. I must have it. Every day, *madre mía*, every day, I must have it.' She heaves a long sigh, pays, and leaves with her six bars of dark chocolate.

El Berro maybe has around two hundred houses built into the hillside. There are terraced lookalike allotments growing almond, olive and orange trees, potatoes and wild oats in a small patch flecked with scarlet poppies. Lungwort-type blue flowers, mellow gorse, silence only interrupted by the flapping wings of a small bird, and a cuckoo.

Back on site, there are new neighbours with a caravan and a little girl. He does all the faffing while putting up an awning. She wants to start cleaning the plastic floor they have just put down. The girl falls off the camping chair and cries. Sticks and metal poles cling and clang. Finally, the table and chairs are set out, ready for food.

But what's this? Inside the caravan, a TV starts to blaze Walt Disney advertisements. The little girl does not want to eat anymore. She is plugged into the drug. All this goes on as I am frying the two white sausages, tomato slices and wild thyme in the new frying pan, and brewing more tea. Then it's off for a walk. I have to get away from the noise of the TV.

Somewhere in the forest I sit on a tree stump and have a cigarette, reflecting on the state of the toilets this morning. Someone had flooded the entire floor with bath bubbles, one toilet was blocked, and another stank vilely of a night-before's excesses. As I stand up, I realize that I've sat on a big lump of sticky tree sap. A patch of solid grey mass is stuck to my bottom. My neighbours will think the worst when I get back! Here now are two extreme bikers expertly crawling slowly downhill where there is no track. My presence goes unnoticed except by some strange-sounding yellow and brown birds and a large fox, standing, staring, sniffing, then disappearing at once.

Back at the tent, I prepare dinner. Fat slices of '*jamón ibérico*', a bit like bacon, go into the pan with whole cloves of garlic, cubes of sweet tomato, topped with fresh rosemary which is abundant in the forest. I have even found the little peppermill. The fresh bread is delicious, sprinkled with a little olive oil. Over several cups of tea, I listen to the cuckoo calling once more, to a moving beam of falling sunlight.

7 May 2006

I am walking up a dried-up river, its white limestone-pebbled bed crunching under my boots as I hear the opening sounds of Smetana's 'Moldau' in my head. What could almost be dolmens must have once made a gushing waterfall at my side. Random river thoughts cross my mind. Is it true that Franco had all the rivers of southern Spain blocked off? So where did all the water go? And where is it now? And wasn't Andalucia his favorite place? so why cut off the water supply? Was this another case of unrequited love ending with some sick revenge? I have not lived in Spain long enough to fathom out any answers and, for now, merely continue to walk along a seemingly endless path.

Finally, I have made my way steadily uphill for three hours along the riverbed and up a the winding path to the top of the mountain that was shrouded in cloud yesterday. Past a huge cave in the craggy limestone rock, past hundreds of little 'fried egg' plants - white petals with a yellow centre - past uncountable pine trees, to the top. Collado Blanco, 1226 metres above sea level.

It's that moment. I have a smoke. The scenery blows

me away. The vast valley stretches to far mists of distance, dense forest below, rocky mountains sticking into the clear blue sky.

Then it strikes me like a bolt of electricity.

Why not follow Laurie Lee's footsteps walking through Spain? Where did he go? What did he do? When was it? I can't remember. Why did he leave? How did he feel? What would the places be like today? Stalking Laurie, a dead poet? I am gripped by both a heavy sense of fear and the tempting scent of adventure. I have a choice: I could just go north and holiday in some cheap campsite by a beach, waiting for the boat back to Britain, booked for the first of June. But now I feel as if the poet's voice is addressing me. He had walked like a pilgrim, lost in a foreign country, with no idea where he would spend the night, living on an ascetic diet. Sometimes he had a few raisins in his pockets, other times he would eat berries growing by the roadside. There is no way I could live like that, without regular strong cups of tea. No way. I like to plan ahead, especially when it comes to spending the night somewhere. Laurie's voice eggs me on though in a sort of 'you can do it, just do it' way. His book is even in my rucksack, getting squashed by the thermos. I find the map of his route. Sixteen hundred miles of a hand-drawn line stretches across the outline of Spain. Have I really got the nerve for this? I begin rereading the story and on the very first page come across Laurie's words of his sense of a 'confident belief in good fortune'. Confidence. That's exactly what I need. I muse on this some more, watching a colony of ravens crowing above some rocks, and the swifts circling above me. They make love in mid-air like the members of that rumoured mile-high club. Apparently the only species who 'do it in the air', and who can stay flying in the air for up to three years!

The wind is freezing. I put the book away and make my way down the mountain. Passing patches of deep-red wild orchids, I wander down, back onto the track. Thankfully, the walk back is all downhill. I notice so many blossoming wild flowers, it is impossible to name them all. Countless bright yellow butterflies, some also coloured blue and orange, are fluttering about where, twenty minutes down the track, the wind is reduced to a gentle breeze, so welcome in the boiling afternoon sun. I sit myself on a rock and have an orange the size of a small child's head for luncheon as well as a hearty sardine sandwich.

What a laugh, the German bikers arriving last night, thea really tidy couple who kiss as they put up a washing line in the semi-dark. This morning, she does all the faffing and shaking with hanging sleeping bags over bike handlebars. He is all white-looking on his return from the showers, a meaty back topped by a round bald head, tiny waxy-white feet.

The night before, my Spanish neighbours were listening to '*fútbol*' on the TV and radio simultaneously but abruptly stopped at 10 p.m. This meant that the bikers spoke a little less loudly at the street corner on my other side, but no, not the Germans, no, the radical bikers.

Back from a radical day's cycling, they showered their bikes down with powerful cold water hoses, then had showers themselves. Two first-aid vans had been waiting for their return all day. As if from nowhere, a man with a huge video camera turned up. Did he film the raiders free-riding? Some kind hand has left glossy magazines and even a DVD outside my tent: 'Adrenaline Hunters', THE OUTDOOR FREERIDE MOVIE. So this is 'free action wildsport', flying over mountain gorges on a mountain bike. People began crowding around the cameraman to get a job in the media or movies or get some slice of the action. Talk, talk. I was frying the two red sausages, spiced with paprika, six cloves of garlic and a tomato in olive oil. Then I sprinkled some wild crushed rosemary over the top and ground loads of black pepper over the lot. I had forgotten to bring a plate and was eating directly from the pan, closely observed by the many bystanders. Well, if there is something I cannot stand, it is being stared at, especially when I am eating. Yet life in a campsite can be very intimate, and everyone knows exactly what everybody else is doing. Eventually, it got too cold to be sitting outside, and I held a Buddha-type yoga position inside the tent for almost an entire hour, fully aware that with the bright glow of my neighbour's extension lighting, my every move was entirely visible to all and sundry.

Once they had all disappeared to the campsite restaurant to party, a late night van turned up without a clue as to where their dedicated patch could be. Five people spilled out of various doors. The women stayed with the van as the men went off into the sparsely-lit dark to explore. I wonder if this is something Spanish, or some symptom from the divided world of men and women, an unspoken law of a 'Hunters and Gatherers society' maybe? Why did the women not go and explore as well? They could have locked the van and joined their boyfriends for a five-minute expedition into the unknown dark. I guess these are unspoken traditions to emphasize who does what in foreign terrain. I found it all a bit old-fashioned. As a single woman, I had learnt the hard lessons of independence over many years. I would have gone to find the toilets first of all and then figured out a good place to camp fairly near to them. Toilets have priority when camping, in my opinion.

To finish the day, here is a final report on the sad state of my face: the tortoise is trying to connect my mouth with my ear which can be tricky during meal times - I do not want a fork stuck in my ear! The two red (paprika) sausages fried with six cloves of garlic, diced tomato, topped with crushed wild rosemary and then covered in mounds of freshly ground pepper were delicious. Over a vast cup of tea, my mind contemplates shy, fingering thoughts forming a plan, focusing on the short future that seems so long. I do not want to be some aimless wanderer, lacking purpose or conviction.

There it is. A decision. No sooner thought than made. I am coming to find you, Laurie. I want see for myself what your eyes saw, what your nose sniffed out, where your feet carried you. Dead or not, I'm on your trail!

8 May 2006

Exploring Andalucia for a few days, looking for caves and letting the road take me, guide me through a patch of life, seems a good plan this morning. I need to chill out, slow myself down, heal that hideously encrusted face.

I am back in the local shop enquiring if there is any boiled pig's head or '*chicharrón*' amongst all the different *chorizos* and *jamónes*. Dumpling woman got there before me and is already armed with her six bars of chocolate.

'No,' she says to me, 'that is not called pig, '*cerdo*', no, it is called '*javali*', wild pig; in the mountains, they live in the mountains, you don't want to meet one in the mountains.'

I had actually heard a most peculiar noise in the forest yesterday. Truly wondering if it was a wild pig and a bit scared, I whistled for the dog who was chasing something somewhere, maybe the pig?

'*¿No chicharrón de javalí?*'

'*No lo tengo*, (I don't have any),' replies the lady shopkeeper looking down with embarrassment. Good grief, so much emotional trauma over a few slices, or not, of boiled pig's head. We talk about the past weekend. The women have not seen a single cyclist and are amazed at my gossip. I learn that there is a school with eleven children but no bank, *farmacia* or doctor. 'But there is a young Dutch couple at the campsite, and two Swedish people,' says the shopkeeper. Indeed, I have seen the young Dutch couple, incredibly tall people looking terribly in love. I wondered if they had an especially long tent. Question: 'What's quick and intense?' Answer: 'Sex in a campsite'.

The women tell me that the village of El Berro, (watercress), has some ice caves where ice was kept over from the winter. Here, in the Parque Natural de Sierra de Espuna, we have two hundred and fifty square kilometres of rugged highlands, a dream for walkers and climbers. In the northwest of the wild park are twenty-six '*Pozos de la Nieve*' (Ice Caves) where, in the olden days, snow was compressed into ice and then taken to the towns in the area. But today I am not going to wander through the limestone formations or forests. Instead, I am off to take a look at the church, 'Ermita de Ntra. SYa de LOS DOLORES'. It is humming with rhythmic encantations, but I cannot join the service because all the dogs of the entire neighbourhood have crowded around Misty and are barking madly. Here are the English words on a small sign near the church door:

The hermitage like talisman against all badly.
This hermitage was granted by Real Order of 18 of
May 1885 like branch of the Parish of San Lazaro
Bishop of the ville of Alhama. The hermitage was
released with a baptism. The invocation of Our Mrs. of
the Dolores is rooted in all the east zone of Spain,
being popularly well-known with the name of 'La

Dolorosa', which ties mainly to the celebrations of Easter.

And is that El Berro celebrated its own processions, emphasizing the one of Friday of Dolores, presided over by the image of the Virgin and surrounded by all its Brotherhood of Daughters of Painful María. The processional route ascended until the calvario where, as it says the parochial newspaper of the time, 'The Saint Cross', would be the rock in where they would be had to crash all evils which they could happen to this religious town.

That is almost the level of my Spanish. I wish. I end up at the beginning of the village. The sign here reads - *Bienvenidos A EL BERRO me pones imposible* - (Welcome to El Berro you take me impossible?). As I am trying to work that one out, I see a poster on a notice board advertising a movie to be screened in Alhama, my next destination. '*Los Monologos de la Vagina de Eve Ensler*' (The Monologues of the Vagina). I don't believe this, and have read it over and over again. Surely this is a bit over the top for around here? I have heard about this film; apparently it is very funny, but I am surprised that the people of this very rural area are keen to see such an upbeat movie. It seems such a contradiction between traditional church values and modern day life.

I am still grappling with trying to find the deeper meaning of it all whilst frying some more fat bacon and slices of crunchy, fresh paprika as well as the daily tomato. I am too rushed for cups of tea as I'm off for a drink with Leif and Inger, a Swedish couple who spoke to me earlier when I was drinking tea and staring at maps spread on the ground all around me.

They have been to over four hundred campsites in

Spain and reckon that this one is the best of the lot. A large swimming pool, a friendly bar, a clean restaurant, very nice staff, all set in stunning terrain. In the summer the couple go north, because it's too hot around here. They show me around their motorhome and two attached tents, full of books, neatly stacked. Hey, Laurie, you would have liked that! Me too. There is even a little vase of wild flowers on the table. The two of them never go back to Sweden, preferring their new life-style. as 'permacampers'. They believe that alcohol is the only remedy to stop the tortoise growing even bigger. Looking at my totally gross growth, Leif, in cool Nordic, true Swedish, unfazable style, says simply, 'We have seen worse.' Then it's off to the pub.

9 May 2006

Last night Leif's wife Inger told me about the hot springs in Zujar. We even found it on my map. Go past Baza, find sign for Zujar. She mentioned a campsite. So today I'm going there.

How are radials different from normal tyres? Ah, the misteriesmysteries in life! I've got two new front tyres. Gripping the road with stick-on speed I sail clean past Lorca. I meant to stop, but I just couldn't. Nor could the Romans who merely used 'Illurco' as a stopover on the road between the Pyrenees and Cadiz. Captured from the Visigoths by the Arabs around AD 780, it became known as Lurka. On the same day that his father, Fernando III, captured Sevilla, 23rd November 1243, Alfonso X El Sabio reclaimed Lorca from the Muslims.

I zoom on and into the small town of Alhama de Murcia on market day. It is Tuesday. Misty and I stock up on tomatoes, paprika, garlic, cucumber, bread, milk, dogfood, water, sardines, cigarettes. We have no time or money to watch the avant-garde movie by Eve Ensler and instead decide to nose around the town. Alhama is busy today. People everywhere, shoving each other with their massive shopping '*rolsers*', large shopping suitcases on wheels, kiss kissing cheeks, kissing babies. Big baths of solid marble have been dug up here, an important archeological site, ten euros. I peer through the windows. The four nights at El Berro has set me back fifty-four euros already, and the finger of economy is beckoning with its crooked joints. A woman carrying a huge blue hydrangea in a pot is asking me about the dog's breed. She talks on rapidly but I don't understand a word. I tell her I like her green sequined shoes. She is off to church, I'm off in the direction of Baza, though I have not yet managed to find a way out of this place. With no direction home, I feel like a rolling stone.

On the road, I meet two young guys from Prague who are taking their camper van to Tarifa, for the surfing.Back home, they I boil some nice hot tea, once I've had a pee in a ditch, very tricky, I nearly fall over and almost pee on my foot at the same time as I realize some lorry driver bloke is not at all asleep high up in his classy cab; no, he is watching me! Thankfully, the good-looking surfers are totally oblivious to the whole thing, comparing their watches, checking miles on maps; they plan to make it to Tarifa by tonight. What an absolutely crazy race, why the hurry? I learn that back home, the guys are ski instructors. Playboys!Aha! Playboys, racing downhill or through several countries to surf in dangerous seas. Maybe that's the way to live, just playing around in the big game. I cannot take these people seriously. Maybe I'm too serious.

In Baza, I cannot find the road to Zujar and have to ask around.

In Zujar, I cannot find the hot springs, and 'The campsite is closed till summer,' says the girl behind the bar, her straight blue-black hair covering exactly half of her face. Her one eye stares at my tortoise. It is a very hot afternoon. 'Stuff hot springs and try Freila for campsite,' the girl elaborates. HerOh God, her one staring eye seems to be talking to my tortoise! I panic and go for a sharp exit.

The campsite near Freila is expensive. I have a *café con leche* while Misty is cooling off in the shade. There is a man staring at me from the bar. I say '*Buenos días*,' and 'Are you from around here,' and 'Pretty hot afternoon,' but he just stares.

I turn my back. When I look round a bit later, he is still staring.

On my way to the toilets, he is still staring.

The toilet is blocked. I have to get out of here.

I drive along and across the massive lake, Embalse del Negratin, turquoise-coloured dream amongst the mountains of the Hoya de Baza. Suddenly, I totally change my mind and do a complete U-turn. Bang. Another decision. Totally on impulse, I am going to go off the road, past half-finished houses looking deserted, towards the lake. The track soon becomes yellow baked earth with dead, bleached bits of grass. I go on. The hot Honda lies quite low on the road, and I hope I am not setting the grass on fire. There is even a warning in the car's instruction manual, not to park the hot car on long grass, because of the fire risk. Maybe there is a point to 4x4s, I reflect, creeping slowly over bumps, deep ditches and small rocks on the road. After about half an hour, there is no track at all. Shock absorbers are very expensive to replace so, eventually, I stop the car and look around. There seems to be no point in going on, and I really cannot take the heat of the boiling car any longer.

Exhausted, I check the perspective of the area.

From where I am here, I can walk down to the lake. This is great! After driving around for nearly two hours, I almost got a headache due to tea shortage. But this place rocks! I have a horribly dried-up cigarette waiting for the kettle to boil. After a large, strong cup of tea, it is time to set up camp. It is very, very windy up here, and the tent literally keeps blowing away as I try to put it up.

Now it's ready for sundown. I am sitting on my fab foldable plastic chair with the dots of nail varnish scattered on it, in the middle of nowhere, overlooking a huge lake surrounded by mountains, waiting for the sun to set right in front of me.

I have seen my first glorious bee-eater, its all yellow back, blue belly and dark beak, head and tail. Wow. There is a distant helicopter humming in the air, and I'm thinking of the Spanish Civil War. Ah, solitude. But why am I doing this again? Ah, yes, of course, why wild-camp? Because it's free! *Gratis*, and because I want to feel free. Free of roads, free of people, free of money worries and snakes in the grass, whatever that sort of free is, that's what I'm after. Laurie was 'affronted by freedom'. I wonder what I will be. Dinner is uneventful and the same as luncheon with the playboys: fresh grainy bread with boiled pig's head, a tomatoe eaten like an apple, and tea, but without the the Polish playboys.

Some shrubby bushes are rustling in the wind, a bird sings, another answers to the falling sun surrounded by a misty diffuse orange hue. Yesterday's egg-shaped clouds have stretched into thin white strips, a gauzy blanket floating over the mountains.

Wild fennel fragrance in the evening air carries the songs of a Spanish skylark, singing me 'good night'.

Now the sun is down and the mountains look all different hues of blue, the light orange blanket covering them gently. God, we are such small little things, no wonder we keep asking for Your help. I hope there's no more snakes. The bloody groundsheet keeps lifting up either side of the sleeping bag; a cold, windy night ahead? I am feeling a bit scared of my solitude, my courage beginning to sink in the face of the strong, billowing winds and the failing light. Now, there are sliced-up slithers of pink strips of cloud in the evening sky, and the mountains are going from charcoal grey to soft black. Behind me, the almost full moon hangs in blue velvet. The wind has slowed down to the baseline gush of night air. Blood-orange background carves out the craggy peaks as the world goes purple and the lark lullabies. A star appears. 'I am in the warm fold of God's loving arm,' I overhear myself thinking.

Then the tent flaps. Misty springs forward and growls.

What's that noise crunching through the night air?

Where's the torch? I grope about in the dark to reach the tent's one pocket. Up flaps another corner of the groundsheet. I must not burn a hole in it. I find the ashtray, kill the fag. Here is the torch. From outside, I hear a definite 'crack'. I am terror-struck.

I find the switch. There it is - a great long stick thrown by the dog to the door of the tent. Did she sense my moment of near panic and is this her idea of how to deal with fear? Get a big stick and defend yourself against invisible things that loudly go 'crack' in the lonely night? I hold my breath, feeling as free as a dazzled rabbit.

Oh God, another 'click'.'crack'. But I'm all right now that I have a stick and a light; come what may I'm ready to fight with my trusted dog at my side. I gingerly stick my head out of the tent to spot the approaching axe-man in the black dark. There is absolutely nobody out there. I can feel myself going off on one and instead concentrate, my mind ranting fear and panic at me, when I manage to trick it by concentrating my thoughts on ant life. instead. Camping brings you closer to nature, naturally, but it brings you especially close to ants. Crawling about almost everywhere, you need to check the ground before pitching the tent to avoid an invasion. Some people even surround their tents with a thick line of coarse salt. I am not sure if it works to keep the ants out. The thing to look for are holes in the ground the size of a child's fingernail. Beware! Soon, the ants will climb out of these little holes in their hundreds, making determined trails to somewhere and then come all the way back. Spanish ants are quite big, about twice the size of a normal Scottish ant. You do not want these ants in your pants, they bite or do something similar, irritating the skin. I like ants. They are a complete mystery to me. Sometimes, the holes in the earth are surrounded by small circular mounds. Maybe the ants have built an underground extension of their sleeping quarters and just brought the spare earth to the top, or what? I wonder, if ants go to sleep, how they sleep. Do ants snore? Do they curl all their legs under and sleep like tiny shiny balls? Do they have caves or tunnels where they roll into a pile or do they sleep in formation like their walking colonnades? Some people say, ants never sleep but just keep busy all the time. Busy doing what exactly? Ah, so much to learn, so little time!

10 May 2006

I wake to bright sunshine and immediately fall asleep again, dreaming of dumpling woman asking me if I had permission to wild-camp, and me giving her the Spanish shrug.

Breakfast is a tin of sardines and stale bread with a big cup of tea. Down by the lake, Misty is swimming like an otter, just for the fun of it, chewing and tearing sticks at random, then rolling on her back on the pebbled shore. I just sit by the edge of the water, wallowing in rejection. By this time I should have had the result of thea writing competition I had entered, but '*nada*', nothing, no prize, no moment of glory, no money. The level of my disappointment stretches in front of me like a long, grey, dead and dried-up snake. Too depressed to go for a walk, I watch the dog diving to catch something out of the water. Another stick? Great, a rock. Now Misty Blue is whining at a dead tree stump stuck in the lake. She cannot rip it up and stares at it bewildered, looking demented.

I want to mope and wallow more, but Misty won't let me. She has brought me five sticks and is now diving for more stones. Too depressed to eat the huge orange, I light another fag. It tastes like horse food. Fish are truly jumping and so is Misty, back into the water.

By 3 p.m. I have taken a hold of myself and, walking around, I practise my diaphragm exercises. The muscle, not the contraceptive device. I learnt this technique from choirsinging. Breathing in to the count of five and blowing the breath out to over twenty is my aim. Also, I flail my arms about wildly in flamenco language gone yoga, making chicken and bear noises. Things you have to do for your voice! But it all helps, especially if you're a smoker. I pee behind a bush and take the washing out of the lake.

By 4 p.m. I've got the kettle on. There is absolutely no shade on this treeless stretch of earth, and I get the pink and orange umbrella out of the car to stick into the ground. There is a very hot wind blowing. I don the silly hat but it takes a major metal hairclip to hold it in place. Now the tea is brewed, I have a nice hot cuppa. 'Fire with fire,' says the homeopath within me, as I burst into tsunamis of fresh sweat, and, bit by bit, cool down. I boil two eggs in the tea water to save on the gas and plan to open the jar of mayonnaise for dinner later.

By 5.30 p.m., the sun is over the yardarm, and I have a cheers inspection, for a proper reflection. It dawns on me that Laurie went to about twenty different places after walking out 'one midsummer morning'. The boat to Britain leaves on the first of June. I have twenty-one days. I worry about visiting twenty places in twenty-one days. How can this be done? I decide to go to 'Hollywood' to try my luck.

I hear weird bird sounds in the distance. Sometimes I wish somebody would invent binoculars for ears. Fat grey clouds linger in front of the sun, but, man, it's still incredibly hot. Fat cumulus clouds are rising in the darkening north. If this is rain coming, the track back up to the road will turn into a river, and I will have to stay on. I will run out of water for tea; then again, there's the lake.

Over dinner, a vast egg mayo sandwich liberally doused in freshly ground black pepper, I watch the ants crawling about doing formation walking. One has this huge seed and keeps trying to balance it home, whilst the others walk by, not giving a damn, called by an invisible, maybe magnetic, force.

'Why don't you guys help this one with the big seed, struggling, perhaps to his death, in the "wrong" direction?' I stare in sheer disbelief at the running ants. Ah well. What can you do? Laurie himself had done plenty of ant-watching. He had followed a track for several days, living on figs and ears of wheat, realizing that never in his life had he felt 'so fat with time, so free of the need to be moving or doing. For hours I could watch some manic ant dragging a piece of orange peel through the grass, pushing and pulling against impossible barriers in a confused and directionless frenzy'.

I notice that I have filthy fingernails like a 'real' wild-camper. By 7 p.m. I realize I have not once looked into a mirror all day. This is something of a record for me, vain lipstick addict that I am. I look at the dried-up ground around me. Where are the ants? Have they gone to sleep? Where are they? I can see none. They have completely disappeared. Weird. I stare at the giraffe for inspiration.

Will tomorrow reveal the new me?

With no fears of the dark?
No fears of not winning?
Of not being good enough?
Tomorrow, the mirror.
Ah, herpetic skin, please get better!

11 May 2006

As it turns out later, I have no recollection of this day whatsoever.

I realize this the day after. The only thing I faintly remember is a fierce screaming in my mind, going, 'I need people! Give me people! I might go mad!'

12 May 2006

Whatever possessed me to wild-camp here I cannot recount as I take the car gingerly back onto the track, hoping I'll make it back to the road. My fingernails are black but hallelujah! the tortoise has shrunk! I can hardly believe the rear-view mirror showing my cleared-up face. Wow, and here now is a cave. I absolutely have to stop to nose about. A door and window are hacked out of the rock; there is even a chimney sticking out of the top. Did we really live like this? And don't we still live like this now, but in caves of concrete? The place is somehow a bit scary. Any moment now I expect athe invisible, mad axeman to come around the corner, threatening me with wild eyes to remove myself at once. I scurry back to the car.

Finally, I am back on a real road. I take the A334 to Seron. It has an Arabian '*castillo*', and camping is at Las Menas, sixteen kilometres up the road. The Sierra de los Filabres reminds me of New Zealand somehow, the Southern Alps. It looks brilliant gothic Transylvanian-type walking country, but I'm off to Gergal. As I go over the mountains on the narrow A1178, there are constant traffic signs of snowflakes, now even the red and white sticks, denoting depths of snow and the trail of the narrow road. The mountains are breathtaking, craggy with patches of fragrant pine forests.

On the top of the Collado de el Conde, 1870 metres, there is a *refugio*, 'Arroyo Berruga'. Further along, another *refugio* at La Hoya, 'Venta Louisa', also 1870 metres. These *refugios* are worth knowing about; you can stay there for free, a bit like mountain rescue huts or bothies in the Highlands of Scotland. I pass the white observatory, 'Calar Alto', 2168 metres above sea level.

It is trying to rain up here and is really, really cold. What a contrast to yesterday's killer heat. But back onto the A92, the Sierra Nevada is rising on my right, as I head off towards Mini Hollywood in the Tabernas desert. Over a hundred Westerns were shot in this south Andalucian desertscape: 'The Good, the Bad and the Ugly', 'The Magnificent Seven', 'A Fistful of Dollars', in the typical spaghetti western genre.

Don't ask me why, but unbelievably I shoot straight past the turn-off. There goes my chance to fancy myself as a bygone movie star. Ah, well. On towards Almeria, I guess.

The town of Almeria became rich from weaving silk produced by the silkworms of the Alpujarras, but it was razed by an earthquake in 1522. The Alcazaba though still rises from the cliffs, and on its northern side are the remains of the Palacio de Almotacin. It houses the 'Ventana de la Odalisca', the Concubine's Window, from which a slave girl leapt to her death after her imprisoned Christian lover had been thrown from it. Oh, dear!

From the port, one can catch the ferry to Morocco.

The county of Almeria is a semi-desert. On my way to

Almuñecar on the E15, I cross four rivers, all dried up, and go past vast ugly plastic greenhouses where all the lovely tomatoes are growing. The entire area between Almeria and Adra is covered in horrendous plastic. Do not go there, it's a living nightmare. As the E15 becomes the N340, the sea crashes against rocks, and cars are splashed with sea spray. After five tunnels (my personal nightmare), I eventually reach Almuñecar.

Hi Laurie, I've made it! I have arrived at my starting point, the end of your journey.
At first sight, the place looks like a typically uninviting agglomeration of apartment blocks. Presently, I am waiting at the Playa de Cristobal for the tourist information to open. The girl inside shows me the position of Laurie Lee's monument on the street plan.

'But I think it is not there. They are building an '*aparcamiento sub-terreno*', underground carpark,' she says, giving me a sympathetic look. There is a peculiar skin blemish on her face too. She says, 'Yes, there is a campsite near, go leave town backwards.' I park the car in the shade, open the large back window for Misty who is guarding the Thursday shopping, and go for a coffee.

The waiter has never seen the monument. As I walk outside to sit on the beach with the *café con leche*, I instead bang it and my head, on the crystal-clean glass door, spilling warm milk into an ominous lookalike post ejaculation stain. The waiter quickly wipes it up and opens the door. Why do I not turn around and ask 'Who cleaned that?' really assertively? I know, it's that smoking moment. Outside, I have a cigarette, wondering superstitiously if the door incident is a dark omen. Maybe the entire trip is doomed to failure.

Back at the car, Misty Blue's head is looking from her

open window. But what's this? Her white nose has gone bright orange. I don't believe it. She has stolen the whole paprika *chorizo*, string and all! That's dinner gone then.

We walk along the promenade towards La Herradura. There is a small monument to 'all those who love sport'. We must have walked in the wrong direction, although I do believe, La Herradura is what used to be Altofaro. There is a lighthouse, '*faro*', nearby, and it is possible, at a push, to swim from there to the edge of Almuñecar. Help me out here, Laurie; there is no Altofaro on my new map. You say it's ten kilometres down the coast, but on your map, it's up the coast. There is a tunnel, not a bridge, in the road between Almuñecar and La Herradura, but nothing of the kind up or down the road.

After one and a half hours I have found the way up to the castle. I reckon Laurie lived either at No. 23 or No. 27 of the Esplanada de San Miguel. Sea view. I take photos. Later I see that he lived near a church, not the castle? The church is in town, no sea views there! Are you laughing at me, Laurie?

What really catches my imagination are the tiny cobblestones everywhere. Hell to walk on in kitten heels, all the narrow old streets covered with them, set into fancy patters.patterns. In the renovated old town centre, there are bleached white ones, set in with dark grey or brown ones. They are everywhere. The town feels a bit depressed but the shops are busy, and there are three bookshops, two clubs, and an internet cafe.

During Laurie's time here, there was one bookshop but it only had four books. He never said what they were. Did his boots crunch and scrape over these pebbled pavements? Do pebbles, like water, hold memories? Laurie speaks of 'rasping pebbles'... I have to stop daydreaming, prioritize, and find a campsite. Also, I am absolutely starving.

After several U-turns, a nice man in a cigarette shop even makes a phone call on my behalf, but I can feel myself coming over all funny. This is serious tea shortage. Somehow, I know there is a campsite somewhere around here, and not the kind man's friend's country hotel. I follow my instinct, and within minutes I screech to an abrupt halt. There it is: 'Camping 318km'. Phew.

And here is a small round man in jeans and a bright pink polo shirt beckoning me in. His office feels like a converted tool shed. He wants thirteen euros per night after studying my passport for twenty minutes.

'Eighteen euros for both of you.'

'But there is only one of me, and the dog!'

'Only one of you, and a dog?'

A grossly large lookalike diamond glistens in his left ear. He looks at me sideways and, deeply in thought, looks a little more at the passport. He looks at me again, then goes outside to the car. Looks at the car. Comes back beaming from ear to ear, apologizing using every single hand, arm, and finger movement from the Spanish gesture language, and laughs at himself.

'The steering wheel,' he makes driving motions, 'it is on the other side!' pointing to the other side.

Relieved, he tells me to come to his house for 'a wine, or a beer', once I have put up my tent. 'I have problems with my wife. You are a *"divorciada"*? My house is here! Over here!' He points more.

There is only space for three tents. It is all occupied. I camp in the car park. Manolo, the pink-shirted *'jefe'* or boss, introduces me to a young bloke, Fernando, and leaves. Fernando asks me to come over for a cup of tea, if I'd like to, later on.

The kettle is on in the back of the car as I put up the tent. I'm going OTT with two teabags in one cup, and I am revived within minutes. What a spectacular bit of all-terrain driving today. Phew. As I am recovering from the extremes of the day, the heat and the cold, the slow and narrow roads and the wide multi-laned motorways, the heights and valleys of the Sierras, I identify another smoking moment. I do know that smoking is very harmful to the body, there is no excuse, and I should know much better, but sometimes, smoking can help you reflect.

I have a cigarette, watching my Spanish cup-a-soup brew, its little croutons blowing up as I smoke.

I miss music a lot; I didn't know I was such an addict. The car radio keeps cutting out and crackling because the aerial got snapped off, and the tape head is so dirty, Sam Cook sounds as if he's under water, plus I only have one tape that works...

Some bread now, and I dive into the croutoned soupfest. It is the foulest thing I have ever tasted but, in pure starving disbelief, I try again. Slimy cubes of sodden baking powder hit my mouth, covered in chicken and asparagus-flavoured goo. Delicately balanced on a small rock, the giraffe falls over. I put it back into my satchel, grab two tomatoes, the *alioli*, whistle for the dog and go see Fernando. He puts the kettle on. Dusk is falling. His neighbour arrives and proceeds to assemble a triangular plastic table. Not speaking, only his hands are visible. I want to rush over to say, 'Man, it fits this way', but I just sit. Fernando places a cup of tea in front of me. He has a table and chairs! I put the tomatoes and garlic mayo on the table.

'The neighbour does not speak much?'

'I think he comes to pray. I'm not really sure.'

An English couple arrives with two dogs. They will not answer to any commands, dying to know what Misty is all about. The couple indulges the dogs' attitudes as if they are a pair of unruly children.

'Stop marking, Oscar,' the woman goes as the dog is off into Fernando's open tent for a wee pee inside. 'Just to let bitch know I was here', or something. Who knows what goes through a dog's mind. Fernando calls softly, 'Oscar!' and the dog emerges, unpeed, rushing off into the undergrowth. Over the tops of the trees I can see vast stretches of savanna in the sunset. The English couple are away into their tent, the dogs pacified at last. The man 'next door' begins to chant to Arabic radio sounds.

'But it is not Friday?' I ask incredulously.

'Yes, today is Friday.' Fernando is completely sure. I'm not. What happened? Have I lost a day or am I on the brink of madness?

'It's not Thursday?' I ask after cleverly rehearsing the names of the days of the week from my Spanish class in my head.

'It is Friday.' Fernando, calm, is totally sure.

Good God, I have truly lost an entire day! This comes as a bit of a shock. But that is how your Friday feeling can kick in, eh, just like that, with a bang. I have a tomatoe and listen to the chanting some more.

Fernando is all set up here, a whole little workshop on his table for cutting bits of rubber to make strips for a fringe, attaching coloured ribbons to multicoloured strings with fancy metal moveable joints.

'For girls, at festivals, they twirl them, it is very pretty.'

I am watching tiny black squirrels rushing up an old tree in front of us. 'Mistee', a rustle through the leaves, and she is back, licking Fernando's knee.

'Maybe my neighbour will make a church there, no?' Fernando grins. We laugh quietly.

I tell Fernando about Laurie Lee. He is a blond rasta, Fernando, not Laurie, with the most graceful movements you'll see in a man, and a smile, when it happens, of the utmost harmony's contentment.

The chanting neighbour leaves.

We light a wee candle and begin to study maps. I learn stuff about beaches he has been to, islands to the north where only tents are allowed, rugged coasts and distant cities.

'I sell them at the festivals. People want these twirly strings.' I forget the French word he uses he uses for them. I may have lost a whole day, but there is still no 'Altofaro' on any of our maps and we cannot puzzle it out. Music starts behind a rickety bar way off. A minute Frenchman in a delectable crumpled shirt joins us smoking buddies later in the night as the music dies. We have a laugh about my never-again-slime-soup experience, and Fernando produces some odd-looking fruits from the trees and bushes around us. I think of Laurie with raisins in his pocket, try and describe his dreamy blue eyes, the high forehead, the elegant nose, the full mouth and fine blond hair to Fernando, but Spanish words sadly fail me.

Back in the tent, I have a goodnight dram all to myself, and fall asleep next to the other vast orange, my planned breakfast.

13 May 2006

I wake up at 5am because I can't see. Like a one-eyed chicken I stare about wildly. Badly stung near my eyebrow, I try and blink a huge swelling away, but it just wants to do victim tortoise talk .. As a result, I can hardly open my eye. Mosquitoes! Damn! Why me?

Fernando arrives at some later time, happily cycling. I decide to eat the orange. Yes, that's right. I had galloping temptation, last night, to ask him to come with me, to sell his string things at the Edinburgh fringe. Was I mad? Something I said? Did I forget that I'm on a mission, have to go it alone, see you later, my friend, the road is my home. Laurie did it on his own and so will I.

I drive off to the wrong Sam Cook song, directly into a dead end of the campsite, before getting back on track...

Back in Almuñecar, population eighteen thousand, as well as numerous French, German, English, Scandinavian speaking tourists. Apartment blocks are rising up next to the rocks where people gathered the night the Spanish(!) destroyer anchored in the bay and blew up a few houses 'by accident'. One can almost hear the duff echoes of explosions bouncing off the rocks.

In July 1936, the bridges had been blown up and, Laurie reckoned, Almuñecar was now cut off. Then he saw that the casino had been burnt out, and outside in the street, 'a grand piano lay with its legs in the air, smouldering gently like a roasted ox'. The peasants and fishermen who had been coming down to Almuñecar for days, now 'openly took over the village, commandeering the houses of suspects and the empty villas of the rich and painting across them their plans for a new millenium. "Here will be the nursery school"; "Here will be the House of Culture"; "Here will be a Sanatorium for Women"; "Workers Respect this House for Agricultural Science"; and "Here will be a training college for girls". Each of the large bold words was painstakingly written in red, a memorandum of a brief and innocent euphoria.'

'For who among the crowds could guess', Laurie goes on, 'that these naive hopes would later be treated as outrage?

'The criminal forces of socialism, which had drawn their slime across the country, were being routed by the soldiers of righteousness, headed by Franco, the "Butcher from Asturias". Thousands of Moorish troops were being flown into Spain every day.'

'The Catholic Kings were the first to drive the Moors from Spain. Now the Catholic generals are bringing them back. The war is over, I think,' were the words of Manolo, Laurie's friend. Suddenly there was a loud hammering on the door, a woman shouting, 'You are saved. Your King has sent you a ship!' Right enough, a boat was waiting on the beach, to take Laurie and his writer friend home. 'No panic,' the smart officer in white had said, 'but the Navy had sent a destroyer from Gibraltar to pick up any British subjects.'

So the end to a year and a half's adventure had come 'with the long arm reaching from home. We could stay of course, but the Civil War was spreading and the captain couldn't guarantee they would be back.'

For Laurie it was the expression on the faces of the villagers which decided him, the hotel fiddler and his friend to make their departure. Once on board, 'the captain welcomed us with a handshake like a squire at a picnic'. Talk of irony. After all the chaos and destruction Laurie had witnessed earlier, the 'stiff upper lip' Britishness must have hit him like a twelve-ton truck.

Later, Laurie stood on deck alone, 'watching Almuñecar grow small and Spain folding itself away. Spain drifted away from me, thunder bright on the horizon, and I left it there, beneath its copper clouds.'

Following Laurie's memories, I spy a few boats lying on a lazy beach, old men playing petanca. Every wave of the sea drags countless 'rasping' pebbles down, then washes them back up. Do, making that rasping sound. I bet they remember?.

Today I must find the monument. I am wandering along the promenade on the other side of the rock with the cross lit up at night. My tourist map tells me this is where it is. After two hours the dog has started limping but there is nothing wrong with her paw. I slowly begin to accept that the tourist information girl was right. There is no monument.

"The grand writer Laurie Lee once passed this way and immortalized the town in his work As I Walked Out One Midsummer Morning and A Rose For Winter"

It is gone.

I feel bereaved, cheated. Watch cars driving underneath

the promenade into a car park. Take disillusioned photos of the building site on top. Man, the very Mayor put up the monument, how can it have just been axed? My mind is having its daily rant; I have to be patient with it, rambling on and on, grumbling attitude at me. Then I can't find the car. But I parked it there!

'No. You obviously didn't. What you should have done...'

'Oh shut up.' My internal dialogue depresses me.

WeThe dog and I are hobbling over some more pebbled pavements in the old town. Just like you imagine the real old Spain with its ingenious drainage pipes and dangling bundles of electrical cables amongst the pots of geraniums on steep steps, tiny balconies, small roofs, and crumbling window ledges.

Why is the dog still limping?

Past a park with exotic birds making weird noises but, instantly curing Misty's limp, we're back at the promenade. There's the car.

Out at sea, a boat in full sail floats by, reminding me of Laurie standing on deck, 'watching Almuñecar grow small and Spain folding itself away' remembering 'the great gold plains, the arid and mythical distances, where the sun rose up like a butcher each morning and left curtains of blood each night'.

Altofaro also remains unfound. Has it been obliterated, exploded, flattened to nothing, or has it just had a change of name, La Herradura for example?

It is here, and Almuñecar where the Civil War started, the key strategic points.

DepressedStill depressed, I drive on to Nerja. Laurie doesn't mention it, but there is a fabulous cave here. A young man outside shows me the pictures of the brochure. Inside the cave are masses of gigantic crystals, different colours, long ones, short ones. 'In the Guinness Book of Records, you know,' he says in his best English. Sadly, it's 2.30 pm, and this is Spain. The cave closed half an hour ago for siesta until 5 pm.

Onwards to Malaga then, and the apartment block monster spreads itself all along the coastal road. Laurie would surely turn in his grave if he saw this place now.

Seventy years ago, he expected Malaga, from its name, 'to be a kind of turreted stronghold, half Saracen, half Corsair-pirate'. Instead, he found 'an untidy city on the banks of a dried up river, facing a modern commercial harbour, the streets full of cafés and slummy bars, and its finest building the post office'. He remarks on the many foreigners present as the 'effeminate Dutch, sandy Germans, mackintoshed Frenchmen, and English debs'. He shared digs in a courtyard with about a dozen families. 'Cooking went on all day at their separate fires, in pots mounted on little stones...the presence of fire was more comforting than the food, which was usually a gruel of unmentionable scraps'. But he 'bedded down...with the mules and wives and children. Honour, not modesty, was what we lived by here'. The courtyard people had come down from the Alpujarras to sell baskets and half Mexican, half Arab style blankets.

Today, Malaga is often ignored by many visitors who go straight from the airport to the Costa del Sol resorts. Malaga is a glitzy port city with its own charms, leafy boulevards, museums, dilapidated old streets and trendy shops. It flourished in the Muslim era but the Christians took over in 1487. By the nineteenth century, Malaga had become a fancy winter resort for the rich. During the Civil War, it was Republican at first but was taken by the

Nationalists in 1937 after being bombed by planes from Italy. Birthplace of Picasso, the Palacio de Buenavista is a major new museum housing many of his works.

A disaster occurred to Laurie during his last days in town - his violin suddenly broke in his hands, 'and the instrument simply fell to pieces'. After trying his hand at being a tourist guide to make a little money, he was saved by a stroke of luck: he met a young German who wondered if he knew anyone who wanted a violin? It belonged to his girlfriend who had dumped him and nobody wanted the violin. He gave it to Laurie for nothing. Just goes to show, there is no such thing as coincidence?

My finances hitting another low, I wonder why I have not got the nerve to get the keyboard and play a few tunes. Low self-esteem and lack of practice? I hack on and even turn off to see Torremolinos after watching the hilarious film 'Torremolinos '73' last summer in Edinburgh. I thought Benidorm is pretty off it but this place takes the biscuit. High hotels and boring, ugly concrete apartment blocks, fish and chips all over, I try to get out as quickly as I zoomed in but of course end up going in the wrong direction. The car, the dog and I are boiling in the heat, but eventually we rejoin the road south.

'The road...followed a beautiful but exhausted shore, seemingly forgotten by the world....San Pedro, Estepona, Marbella and Fuengirola...They were saltfish villages, thin-ribbed, sea-hating, cursing their place in the sun. At that time one could have bought the coast for a shilling. Not Emperors could buy it now'. Oh, Laurie.

We arrive in Algeciras, the major port linking Spain with Africa, as well as an industrial town producing toxic smells for miles around. It is also a big fishing port and a major centre for drug smuggling.

Laurie goes on about Algeciras as 'having a potency and charm which I'd found nowhere else...a scruffy little town built round an open drain and smelling of fruit skins and rotten fish. There were a few brawling bars and modest brothels, otherwise the chief activity was smuggling'.

Algeciras was taken from the Merenids of Morocco by Alfonso XI in 1344 but later razed to the ground by Mohammed V of Granada. In 1704, after Gibraltar was taken by the British, its people came to live in Algeciras.

You can leave your car and store surplus luggage, if you are going to Morocco, at the huge port. I remember doing just that with Louise a few years ago. We spent one night in Tangier's old town and swore that we would never return. The whole thing had been a bit of a nightmare, and she ended up sleeping with a knife under her pillow whilst I was terrified of a cockroach in the filthy shower tray. All night long there was a terrible screaming in the street below, and our imaginations ran wild.

Laurie got out his fiddle one night, and was 'invited to serenade a man's invalid mistress'. He was rewarded with 'a wristwatch which ticked madly for an hour and then exploded in a shower of wheels'. Laurie was 'half in love with Algeciras and its miniature villanies' but he had planned to follow the coast around Spain. I had just driven the journey in a couple of hours which had taken Laurie five days. 'The road rippled beforbefore me, and distant villages in the mountains shone like salt on silk'.

But here's looking at you, Gibraltar. Laurie thought he'd drop in for a cup of afternoon tea, and was carried across by an old paddle wheel ferry. He found it like Torquay - 'the same helmeted police, tall angular women, and a cosy smell of provincial groceries... the atmosphere of home depended on white bread, soap, and soup-squares'. At Customs, he 'was put to one side like an infected apple'. Seeing he was broke and travelled only with his fiddle, the authorities regarded him with suspicion. Phone calls were made, and he ended up sleeping in the police station, playing dominoes with the prisoners. But after a few days of bacon and eggs, he left the island, saying it was 'like escaping from an elder brother in charge of an open jail'.

I have no wish to go thereto an open jail and move on to Tarifa. As I drive up the winding road, I do not see Laurie's 'vultures moving like the blades of electric fans'. Instead, I see a forest of hundreds of three-bladed wind turbines, whirring and humming; it is all a bit eerie.

Through the newly-built and not yet inhabited rows of houses, I go down into Tarifa's old town, the *mudéjar* Puerta de Jerez, built after the Reconquista. There is a busy little market just packing up, a fifteenth century church, closed, and the streets, yes, Laurie, 'still skulking behind its Arab walls. Once a Barbary stronghold and master of the Straits..' Tarifa takes its name from Tarif ibn Malik who led a Muslim raid in 710, the year before the main Islamic invasion. The Christians took the town in 1292.

It is hard to know if the gun windows in the lookout towers were used for the Civil War, and only months after its resolution, for World War II. They are broken and crumbling now, and permission to enter is discouraged by a very tall, sturdy fence. Laurie could see Tangier from here. 'I watched the sun go down, almost audibly, into a gulf of purple. In the distant dusk one saw the orange smudge of Tangier break into little lights'.

A sign at the *puerto* – harbour - reads 'You are in Tarifa, the SOUTHEST point of Europe'. I have a tin of sardines for some late luncheon.

Back in town, there are trendy little shops and bars by the dozen as well as at least three 'kite schools'. The surf here is ideal for windsurfing, with huge kites. As the rucksacked hippies and rich boys in convertible cars compete for space in the small streets with numerous camper vans, all busy trying to outcool each other, I take off to Punta Paloma. No whale- or dolphin-watching for me. A drive through a military zone -'No Entry - Verboten' - comes to an abrupt end when a soldier leaps out of the undergrowth to inspect me, my car, my dog who is barking madly. '*No pasa nada*,' he says, roughly translated this means 'OK' after regarding the organised camping chaos inside the car. I go on but find nothing for wild-camping. The ground slopes steeply everywhere, and the dense undergrowth appears quite unforgiving. I find a tiny excellent-looking bar, but it is is closed. So I have to turn back. A different soldier salutes me and opens the roadblock.

At 'Punta Paloma' camping ground dogs are allowed and I see the site is surrounded by pale-brown, large-horned cows, all wearing bells the size of flowerpots. There is an aroma of cows, pine trees and purple flowers in the air, topped with the incessant chirpings of innumerable sparrows. It is dinner time, so out comes a tomatoe, a small tin of tuna and the end of the bread, followed by several cups of tea. I am thinking of Laurie leaving home that fateful midsummer morning after a 'heavy breakfast' his mother cooked for him, with only a tin of treacle biscuits and a piece of cheese in his pocket. On his second day, after sleeping in a ditch, he had to beg 'a screw of tea' and then wait an hour for the spring water to boil in the can. I live in luxury in comparison. On his first day in Spain, Laurie bought some bread and fruit, but the next day he just had a few wild grapes which he ate green, as well as the remains of 'a patch of beans'. I hate to think how this could have affected his digestion.

The cow bells jingle and jangle all night. Do cows not sleep or do their bells ring with every breath they take? Wind rushes through the tall pine tops. Bits of twigs fall onto the tent making little clicking noises as the mosquitoes start working on me. They got my left hand earlier and it has now swollen up to the size of a boxing glove. I have done seven scary tunnels up to now (they all have names) and seen many rivers, all of them dried up. Drifting off to sleep, I no longer feel frightened of 'the unknown', of my own courage or the lack of it, realizing that the tortoise had been the expression of that anticipation all along. I resolve to just 'go with it' like Laurie did, not knowing where I would stay the next night or the ones after that but merely trusting in good fortune.

14 May 2006

After tea and sardines, I am off to the showers.

A large wordless woman is armed with a powerful hosepipe. She is cleaning the toilets. Jets of water shoot over the showers, rows of sinks, tiled walls, toilets and floors. A huge spider lies dying in a puddle. There is no toilet paper; just as well I have brought my own. Unlike Manolo's campsite - with toilet paper and electricity to charge up Fernando's phone, and a loudly-singing, showering Frenchman - this is almost like something out of the Cuckoo's Nest. Nurse Ratchet of the Hosepipe, Spiderkiller extraordinaire.

The tortoise has almost totally gone, with only one final, small, dry flake remaining. Instead, I now have what looks like a giant red wine stain on my chin. Hurray - it's been one month of tortoise torture, but the end is in sight.

I am recalling yesterday afternoon's heat when I imagined I could hear the rush of the surf calling. On the beach, the kiters were gliding over and slicing through the white crested waves. Gaudy-coloured kites graced the air with their clever trickery; there must have been nearly a hundred of them. I had a tomatoe and tea from the thermos. It was a bit disgusting.

In the distant mountains, the forest of windmills was wheeling on. Any minute now Don Quixote himself might show up on the mountains to fight the windmills. 'They are evil white riders that must be slain,' he would exclaim, jumping from his horse and running towards them, with Pancho going, 'No, man - they're just windmills with white sails!' Don Quixote raved on regardless.

A shiny black beetle the size of my small finger was fast approaching. I was sitting in the dunes to avoid being sandblasted by the sharp winds coming directly from the Moroccan mountains and deserts. Hot sand was blowing about a foot high like thousands of tiny bits of flying glass. I found a knife stuck into the sand. Good blade, serrated edge, and now it was mine. The beetle had dug its head into the sand again and again - why? What food could have been hidden under a pile of sand? Or was it just trying to get away from the sun? Why did it not just rest in the shade of some leaf?

If this beetle had been a little bigger it could have posed as a small scorpion. Scared, I sent it flying into the stunted, shrubby, pined undergrowth with a flick of your book, Laurie. Sorry.

The verbascum was in full flower; the tall fennel fragrant; vetch with red flowers was climbing; the stunted pines growing sideways, their shape determined by the constant strong winds. There were millions of blue flowers, some looked like miniature geraniums.

Then it happened.

Dream man walked by and stopped to stare at me from a short distance away. I stared back from behind my shades, wanting to make hot passionate love instantly, but I had gone blank on the international sign language for 'what, me?' So nothing happened for delicious ages until he finally turned away. Seeing I am not in the business of following wild strangers into flowering forests, I had a cigarette. Had these kinds of moments been made for cigarettes? Who remembers Albert King singing,

'when the road you're travelling on
gets too long to carry on
and you need some company who really cares,
turn around, turn around, turn around, and I'll be there,
like a road, like a road,
leading home'?

That's how dream man had turned around.

But I was tracing Laurie's footsteps. That's the only man I would follow, staying confident and on the case. I imagined I could see him, in my mind's eye, making his way up the winding road crossing the mountains.

Crossing the Strait of Gibraltar in a small overloaded boat is very dangerous. Yet hundreds of people try to gain illegal entry into Spain across the treacherous strait from Morocco and other African countries every year. They die when their boats capsize or they cannot swim the few hundred yards to the beach after their boats have dumped them. Many bodies are washed up. Many would-be immigrants to Spain are intercepted by coastguard or police and sent back. No one has exact numbers. Spanish police reckon they only managed to catch fifteen per cent of illegal immigrants in 1999. Are the others dead or in Spain? Tarifa and Algeciras are favourite drop-off points for migrants who pay at least twelve hundred euros for the risky trip. I can see Africa from the sand dune I have climbed, but the sea looks forbidding. Deep and rough.

Back at the campsite, new French neighbours spoke German with me, discussing world politics, what they had eaten, and dogs. After listening to what they had feasted on, I was starving. A young Spanish couple had put up their tent hours ago and not emerged from it since. Should we be concerned? I wandered off to get some water. A man was staring at a tiny hole in a drystone wall with a camera. Was he studying spiders, or perhaps minute flowers? Later, he was checking me out, in my small tent, smoking. At least I had some lipstick on which almost matched the 'wine stain'. Surely, the last remaining tortoise flake would fall off by morning?

The belled cows had gone. Someone was practising drumming, badly. The French couple was back from having eaten more, praising some restaurant back in the town.

'The roads, the tunnels, all brand new, we have nothing like that in France,' the French guy remarked on travelling in Spain.

'But you have the highest bridge in the world,' I responded.

'It is nothing. Yes, we have it. But we go out on strike or to protest and even when we go out to vote, the government takes no notice.' His wife nodded and sighed.

'Spanish men piss anywhere,' he went on, 'against walls, skips, lamp posts, dustbins, drainpipes, fallen over trees, sheds, fences. What do the women do? Crouch in ditches, risking to pee on a shoe or do they simply ask for the *aseos*?'

His wife and I exchanged silent glances as he rambled on.

'Ah, the English do not like that word, it sounds too much like "ass", huh?'

His wife and I had feigned ignorance as he prattled on some more.

Vodaphone had just texted me 'Welcome to Morocco please use international dialling code to call Spain', but rather than indulge in a daily rant, after all I was IN Spain, not Morocco, I went off to my tent. A huge creepy-crawly was clinging to the insect door and I hoped that it would not crawl up my trouser leg.

Blankly staring at dark night-time trees, I suddenly realized that my insecure feelings of 'leaving', or wanting to be 'rescued' by someone, a friend, a lover, to come home, had gone. I was looking ahead now, ready for freedom.

Laurie started out 'with a confident belief in good fortune', but his first day alone 'steadily declined in excitement and vigour...Through the solitary morning and afternoon I found myself longing for some opposition or rescue, for the sound of hurrying footsteps coming after me and family voices calling me back. None came. I was free. I was affronted by freedom. The day's silence said, Go where you will. It's all yours. You asked for it. It's up to you now. You're on your own and nobody's going to stop you...I might have turned back then if it hadn't been for my brothers, but I couldn't have borne the look on their faces. So I got off the wall and went on my way'.

For me too, it is time to move on.

I had dreamt about the gifts from friends for my journey, a yellow plastic folding chair, lifesaver for campers with backache, now covered in small blobs of multi-coloured nail varnish; a pocket knife that could saw down small trees; a gadgety pair of pliers for fixing cars; a wind-up torch indispensable for night-time pursuits; binoculars; a compass; and a silly hat for avoiding sunstroke.

Someone had even given me 'his eyes' for the journey.

Today, in one month, I shall be fifty-four. If I am spared.

I am musing more over my morning cup of tea about yesterday's conversation with the French couple. They have different French accents. His German is better than hers. She has fiery red hair. This morning, the man is showing off his 'I don't give a damn' walk balancing his pot belly, and sweetly signalling '*silencio*' as his wife is still asleep. It is 10.30 am as he goes off to lie in the sun and watch me through slitted eyes.

I have another cup of tea, wash the car with cold water, dry it with toilet paper, pack up the tent, and get on the road.

Spanish men drive cars like bullfighters.

Sometimes I drive my Honda Civic like a little red racer, other times I drive like a grandmother, slowly, saving petrol and checking out the terrain. A lot of building is going on on the outskirts of town.

A lover of cranes, the one-armed giants standing on one leg, extending the beam of economic boom, checking angles, perspectives, setting down, lifting, rolling and turning for the collectives, gracing skylines with objectives, I wonder about the new empty houses. As the road curves up and away from Tarifa, I see more ghostly closed shutters. Who is going to live in all these apartments, '*Alquila*' - for rent, '*Se Vende*' - for sale?

I'm off to Cadiz.

On the way I realize that I totally forgot to take a picture of Tarifa. I find a great clump of old-men's-ears cactus covered in pale yellow flowers by the roadside and take my one photo of the day. Onwards and upwards, I travel through a sea of white wind turbines, then huge eucalyptus trees swaying in the wind and, suddenly, there is a stork! Have not seen a stork since childhood when people believed that a stork nesting on the roof brought good luck and prosperity to all and sundry under that roof...

Did Laurie walk the narrow roads along the coast or come along what is now the A340, seeing that 'the dizzy sweep of the water gave me a feeling of vertigo, so that I kept carefully to the middle of the road'? He 'spent almost a week in this Arizona-type landscape. Between the mountains and the sea, the country was dried-up prairie, dun-coloured, smoking with dust. Thin wiry grass bent to the day-long winds which covered them with a ghostly film of salt'.

Unlike Laurie I have no intention of sleeping in a hilltop cemetery and, after about an hour, I arrive in Cadiz. It feels like a Sunday but maybe it is a bank holiday because this is actually Monday. Everybody is off to the beach, carrying beach chairs, towels, cool boxes, pushing pushchairs laden with beach umbrellas; even the babies are wearing shades. Traffic chaos rules and there is absolutely nowhere to park.

Cadiz was founded in 1100BC and may be the oldest city in Europe. The Phoenicians called it 'Gadir' and to this day the people of Cadiz are referred to as '*gaditanos*'. The Romans had a naval base here and apparently loved the food, the women and the music. But the town faded and was taken from the Muslims in 1262. After Columbus's trips to America it began to blossom once more; he started his second and fourth journey from here. In 1587, Sir Francis Drake 'singed the King of Spain's beard' with a raid on the harbour that delayed the Armada. In the eighteenth century, the city prospered due to trade with the Americas, but the loss of the colonies a century later brought serious economic decline and, to this day, Cadiz has one of Spain's highest unemployment levels.

Situated on the head of a peninsula surrounded by desolate coastal marshes, the old city centre reminds one of eighteenth century decayed grandeur, getting slowly restored.

I park illegally on a pavement to take a picture of two huge unidentified trees. Louise had eaten the seeds from one of these trees on our trip a few years earlier only to become violently sick with some gushing digestive disorder. Homeopaths on holiday, say no more. I'll send her the picture.

Meantime, I'm heading for Jerez de la Frontera, just thirty-seven kilometres up the road. My friend and I had travelled here also on our mad search for Dolmens. The place has changed beyond recognition in the last four years, or maybe I have a changed point of view. The station still looks like an Arabic prayer mat and I spot some excellent graffiti nearby. Many roads are blocked off and, bit by bit, I see why. I have just walked into the *Feria del Caballo* (Horse Fair). Here are horses and carriages decked out with bells. Over there, girls and mothers are donning fabulous flamenco dresses of fantasmal colours. A family spills out of a car all decked out in white and blue, like Manchester City supporters.

Jerez is at the heart of the Seville-Cadiz axis where flamenco began. It is the hotbed of flamenco, and here one can find the Andalucian Flamenco Centre which is like a flamenco museum, library and school. Also, there is the Royal Andalucian School of Equestrian Art. The sleek horses and elegant riders are trained in specialist dressage, and the horses learn to 'dance' in Andalucia's 'horse capital'.

So Jerez is not just famous for its sherry, although this is what made the city rich. One can almost smell the abundant affluence from the wide streets, old mansions and well-heeled inhabitants. The Muslims called the town 'Scheris' from which 'Jerez' and 'Sherry' are derived. This drink was already famed in Britain during Shakespearen times.

Trying to find my way out of town, I end up at the zoo, twice. The place is packed with more people, everyone and their grandmother is out today. The radio says it is thirty-two degrees in Seville which is where I'm heading next. Already my shirt is soaked in sweat as the heat is ever rising.

I drive past ripe yellow cornfields and spot another stork, on the nest! It is now thirty-three degrees in the shade, but I am not in the shade. Near Las Cabezas de San Juan, I kid you not, this is not a fiery delusion of sunstroke, I truly spy four vast eagles circling in the blue sky. I immediately have a cigarette. The upturned wingtips are unmistakable. What a sight!

But the road beckons once more. I am about ninety kilometres out of Seville and push on to reach my next destination. I reckon all the people are either in Jerez to fiesta the day away or in Cadiz on the beach as Seville's town centre is almost deserted. The only people left in the Calle de la Paz (Street of Peace) are coach drivers and tired-looking car park attendants. Blond tourists with big shades sitting on horse-drawn carriages are taking in the fabulous architecture of the imposing buildings, hugely wide streets lined with endless blue flowering Jacaranda trees.

I liked the guys liking me at the petrol station, as I'm coming into town, I'm and buying the petrol – God, it's so hot, they're so cool - and I have this big creamy nutty-topped ice cream cone.

'Is it far to the centre?' I ask, knowing that the question has first to be repeated as a statement, then discussed and regarded from every angle, before any answer becomes likely. The discourse of any Spanish conversation seems to run along those rules.

'Far to the centre?' says one guy, maybe considering all aspects of the term 'far' before making a decision. 'No. It is not far. The centre of the town? Five minutes!'

'Less than five. The town centre? Definitely less than five,' replies the other guy, trying to outdo the first. They chatter on between themselves. The time to the town centre depends on how fast I drive, how much traffic there is, what time of day we are looking. I am aware of all this but I am grateful for the shade and the enthusiasm of the two men, happy to have their afternoon boredom relieved by the chance of a stimulating conversation. I am sharpening my attitude as they sharpen their conversation. Eventually, they agree that in my case it will take between two and four minutes to reach the centre. They are smiling in unison, eyeing me up unpeeling the cardboard-clad ice cream.

Wrappers! I lick the ice cream, having flicked the top wrapping off easily with a long fingernail. I have been a nail-biter until the age of thirty-three. I bit my nails to the very core of fingertip pain. Never, in all those years, did I have the ability to slide a fingernail under a bit of wrapping to effect an opening tear. I would use my teeth instead. But I have cultivated fingernails for twenty years now and deftly deal with the rest of the tough ice cream wrapper. Licking and crunching greedily at the treat, trying to prevent it melting even faster, I can feel some of it dribbling down my chin and have to wipe it with the back of my other hand. The young men stare at me. Suddenly self-conscious to the point of embarrassment, I leave, the guys wishing me a '*'bonbuen viaje*', good journey. I take the car back onto the road, crunching away at the gigantic cone, surveying the scene over the steering wheel, careful not to let any ice cream drip onto my trousers.

Friends of mine lived here for twelve years. They told me about the '*barrios*', or districts of the city. One '*barrio*' - the '*triana*'?- is the biggest for scoring drugs, internationally famous for hard drugs. At the time, they lived in the '*barrio*' next door. In a place with a gigantic atrium, open-air indoor-garden type thing, gurgling fountain, blossoming plants, eight bedrooms, and nineteen cats.

My friends had told me that Seville is a party town more than any other place in the whole of Spain. People finish work around 8 pm but they do not go home. Instead, they meet in small bars, have some wine or beers and '*tapas*', small glazed terracotta dishes usually found underneath flowerpots, filled with olives, slices of cheese and '*jamón*' or soupy stews, '*fabadas*', eaten with chunks of crispy white bread. After some more drinking, the people start spontaneously dancing '*sevillanas*' in the streets. This is a style of flamenco dancing involving complicated footwork. My friends told me flamenco is like flirting and 'if it is not in the blood you can never learn it'. They also told me how, off for a Sunday walk by the river at one time, they were suddenly spread-eagled against a wall by the Guardia, fierce police officers, usually wearing black shades, to be searched for drugs.

I have no intention of stopping here. Seville in heated, slumbering Monday siesta, I think not. This is not the time to explore city sleek or old town back streets. Shutters are down, awnings cover balconies to keep out the light and heat. Dogs die in hot cars or burn their paws on melting pavements. But one can smell the style and pride of the city. After Columbus found the Americas in1492, Seville became really rich and, to this day, there seems to be something in the air. Columbus is said to be buried here, in a tomb in the cathedral, his remains having been brought over from Cuba in 1899. Yet no one is totally sure if his real remains were actually lost somewhere in the Caribbean. Ah, Cristobal. Some say, he was actually half-Italian and half-Portugese.

In the cathedral there is also a large Murillo painting of the vision of St Anthony of Padua, but guess what. A pile of thieving clowns cut the saint out of the canvas, probably deftly rolled him up, stuck him under an arm, and walked out. But he was found in New York and replaced back in the picture. I wonder vaguely if, on searching the canvas, one would discover telltale cover-up paint jobs or odd knife marks. Probably not.

I give the dog a drink. The water in the plastic bottle is almost hot enough for a cup of tea. But the dog drinks it anyway. Good girl, Misty.

On the way out of town, I simply cannot believe it.

In Jamaica, ten years ago, you could not buy a bottle of Coke. Pepsi only. Foul-tasting 'Warm or Cold' Guinness, yes, but Coke? No. Only Pepsi. I kid you not. As I'm leaving town, trying to find signposts that don't say 'Madrid', I come across the most incredible sight. Near the airport, here they are, two factories, right next to each other, repeat, right next to each other; one says 'Coca Cola', the other 'Pepsi', the gigantic signs of the world leaders stretching sky-high.

There is also a little sign showing the way to a campsite nearby. But I want to get some more diastancedistance behind me and get back on the A4. I resist the temptation to visit Las Nieves (The Snows?) just for the irony of it being so boiling hot, and anyway, I have to stay on the trail. Laurie did not tell whether he stopped at Carmona or Ecija, between Seville and Cordoba, so who is to know? Maybe he traipsed through the fields and country lanes in the searing heat? He probably had no other choice. I, however, am on a red and white snake mapped out on paper, showing the fastest route to Cordoba, as well as a small triangle, meaning 'camping near here'. Hurray! So just before Cordoba, off I go at exit 434 to 'La Carlotta' campsite.

The campsite 'Carlos III' is quite large and at first sight full of huge stationary caravans. The pool is not open as it is not yet summer, I am told. There is the constant whirr of distant traffic, and I decide instantly that I will not stay for three nights, even at a fifteen per cent discount. The nice young man gives me a sticker for the car which will be handy to cover up a growing rust spot. I can feel an insane-looking grin spreading across my face as I put up the tent. This campsite is very near a place called 'La Paz'. First the huge Calle de la Paz in Sevilla, now this. Paz means 'peace'.

'Increase the peace!' my babbling mind rambles on. It's been a hot day, and '*autovas*' (motorways) and city life are beginning to get to me.

I have a cup of tea.

Today I have seen altogether FIVE EAGLES, two storks, one on a nest, a black-winged tern or what looked like one, two little white egrets, sparrows, crested larks, a large falcon-type raptor, and now there are flocks of tiny goldfinches fluttering in the trees above. Every tent pitch has two trees, probably planted for shade. But it is 9 pm and biting time. Covered in lemon oil spray stuff, I begin to fold the maps away to save them from the night dew.

After Misty's nightly tick inspection, I can reveal that she has a mosquito bite in her EAR! She cannot scratch it because she thinks there is something wrong with her front paw and thus would fall over if she tried to support herself on it. I can see nothing wrong at all. I ask her, if she remembers the squished turquoise-scaled lizard on the road up to the *cementerio* (graveyard) in El Berro and she cocks her head sideways.

Oof, it stank. Or maybe it was the graveyard, not the lizard. In Spanish graveyards, coffins are packed, four high, into thick walls. There are pictures of the deceased on the front and flowers.

'Could I live in the small village?' I asked myself, but the answer was 'No, not for good.'

'What about Almuñecar?'

'Yes, in the old town. I could live there.'

'Or how about Tarifa?'

'No, too windy, too many folks trying to be trendy.'

'Algeciras?'

'No way.' Not since I had witnessed an illegal immigrant being discovered under a lorry and savagely beaten with sticks.

'Cadiz?' Yes, I could live there. The 'city of 'the white fish hook city'bay' as named by Laurie has the wonderful flair of a 'happening' university city. Yet after this morning's incident, I might change my mind. I had parked in front of a garage exit to avoid double parking, parking was completely impossible, to rapidly get the last cash from a hole-in-the-wall money machine across the busy road. As I grabbed my card and the notes, I noticed an old lady leaning into the open window of my car, pressing the hooter frantically. Misty did nothing! Another old lady with identical short curls sat in her car, also hooting merrily, having emerged from the garage. I called across the wide street heaving with traffic, pointing at my head, to say 'that's my car, and I'm coming over this second', but they carried on hooting madly. I expertly dodged the wild traffic and apologized. For goodness sake, a minute's delay cannot be that upsetting? I gave them the shrug and drove off. No, maybe I could not live here after all.

'Jerez?' In a word, no. Too small, too sherried and growing suburbias too fast. Not me.

'Gibraltar?' Under no circumstance. I love Laurie's tongue-in-cheek humour on Gibraltar. He never did get to take 'tea and toast' in the 'colony'. Instead, he was kept in a police cell because he had no money!

Through the treetops I can see pink clouds in the west. The birds have gone to bed. The traffic rushes on. Being alone is the ultimate luxury, but being without any kind of company takes courage. I feel like an urban hermit, one minute I take to the hills to think and contemplate, the next I'm in some odd town doing a Victor Meldrew attitude to anyone and anything. I make more tea and prepare dinner; a tomato, half a jar of white beans, raw garlic, and an entire tin of three fat sardines.

At 10 pm it is still thunderstorm hot and I am dabbing my mosquito bites with whisky. Have just discovered that the torch can stand up on its own. This is pleasing me no end as it means I can hold my pen in one hand and my notebook in the other. Earlier it was a struggle, trying to hold on to the torch as well. I got mad and even switched it off but then I almost drank the ashtray, believing it to be the unbreakable whisky cup. I have just decided what to wear tomorrow, so that's a great relief. Flared jeans, red flamenco shoes, purple fishnet socks, black shirt with red buttons. I do not want Trinny and Susannah suddenly slipping up to me from nowhere checking my style, to find me in flat old sandals, dirty and badly fitting cut-off jeans and a light-blue T-shirt stained on the front with bright red lipstick!

The main thing is that the tortoise has gone. Hurray! I don't even care about mosquito bites (nine), ouch. I cannot understand how the stench of my feet has not deterred them. I turn off the light and have a smoke to help drive them away. I dimly remember sweating my way through sierras.

Frogs have started up somewhere in the distance. Croaking and quarking, they'll be stalked by storks tomorrow.

15 May 2006

Have spent the worst night from hell in the tent, being bitten painfully by swarms of insects or maybe by one really really hungry one, again and again, was only part of it. Every time I heard the familiar zzzzzh I would slap about wildly trying to kill my assassin only to find that the bright white campsite light was shining directly at my site. I was in a mosquito magnet nightmare! Nothing could be done. I was trapped by bright light.

I woke up Mr Whyte and Mr Mackay, the whisky people, for a cheers inspection for I had nothing to be cheery about at all. The term 'desperate measures' took on a whole new meaning. Together, we tried to smoke and squish out the enemy, listening to lorries droning by through the night until the dawn chorus finally lulled us to sleep.

Now, at 9 am, someone is shooting at rabbits or something - mosquitoes?- right next to the fenced hedge. Where do mosquitoes go during the day? To live by muddy waters in froggy swamps or in fat hedges? Misty cannot think about anything; she is terror-struck by the fired shots and has got herself stuck in the large sleeve of the fluffy grey jumper. It is now a shivering heap in the corner of the tent. But we have to go on, so I pack up the tent in the melting morning sun.

Once the shooting has stopped, things feel quite peaceful, the traffic has died down, and the goldfinches zwitscher.

Being a driven woman, I get driving. Up near the almost unfindable Madina al Zara, I see a stork gliding the skies. I am contemplating the noises from the Dutch tent, making love, her moaning quite tunefully without change to climax, him occasionally sighing or grunting. They were probably just going over their accounts. My mind should stop making assumptions. Yet life in a campsite is awfully revealing.

I recount the soldier-type English-looking guy with his two small horrible snappy, yappy doglets who came to check me out last night, the moment I had the tent up, the dog on the washing line. Well, tied to a tree with the washing line. Is it a territory thing with men or what? The way they come sniffing around as soon as there's a new arrival, a 'new kid on the block'. I never saw any women doing it.

The mind muddled with musings, I, of course, take the wrong turn and end up in Cordoba. After miles of green and yellow patchwork hills, Cordoba at first sight seems busy and large with a pretty mad one-way system.

It is Monday. I'm back on track to find the Medina Azahara. I park at the palace, eight kilometres out of town, and take the dog for a walk in the dried up countryside, before venturing into the Medina Azahara, open Tuesdays to Sundays.

It is Monday.

It is closed.

It was built in 936, and by 945 Abd ar-Rahman III had moved into the new city. But during the caliphate's collapse between 1010 and 1013, the Medina Azahara was wrecked by the Berbers. Today, less than one-tenth of the city has been excavated, and only about a quarter is available for sightseeing, except on Mondays. I peek over the wall opposite the car park to spy out some massive horseshoe arches, but I cannot figure out if the relics are of a great hall for military parades, or a mosque. Other visitors arrive by car and wander about dumbfounded, as there is no way in. I'm off, back to Cordoba.

Initially a Roman colony, Cordoba was a major Roman cultural centre and both Seneca and Lucan were born here. But in 711 it was overcome by Islamic invaders. When Al-Andalus was at its peak, Cordoba was its capital. Standing on a curve of the Río Gualdalquivir, Cordoba was the biggest city in Western Europe during the reign of Abd ar-Rahman III. Between 100,000 and 500,000 people lived here at that time. The city had many mosques, libraries, observatories, *patios*, aqueducts and a university as well as many skilled craftsmen working with leather, metal, textiles and glazed tiles. Cordoba became a place of pilgrimage for Muslims who could not make it to Mecca or Jerusalem.

The Mezquita was founded in 785 on a church site divided between Muslims and Christians. Apparently, the Christians were bought out, and building began, to last into the 960s with various extensions over the centuries. Today, however, the Mezquita's final Islamic structure has one large alteration which caused cultural shocks to some. In the very centre of the building there is a sixteenth century cathedral, surrounded by the

Islamic aisles, pillars and arches. The red brick and white stone stripes of the famous rows of two-tier arches are inspired like the fabulous mosaics and rich stucco. Yet what possessed the Christians in the sixteenth century to rip out the centre so that a cathedral could be built right there? My big sister complained about dust on the '*retablo*' or altar, when she visited here in the autumn.
'I have paid seven euros to get in here and there is dust lying around! This is not acceptable.' She was black affronted. This could of course have been caused by the Christian-Islamic culture shock. After all, Carlos I, too, is said to have gone mad at the church authorities, saying, 'You have destroyed something that was unique in the world.'

Is the 'Mezquita-Catedral', as it is often described, possibly supposed to be a symbol of religious tolerance?

Wandering around the streets, Misty and I check out the Puente Romano (Roman Bridge) crossing the Guadalquivir, to have a look at the restored Islamic water wheel. Then it's back towards the Mezquita, past lots of '*patios*', atrium-like indoor gardens. These are usually hidden behind heavy doors, but during May, it is possible to visit some of them to get a glimpse of the heavenly peace and quiet, surrounded by glorious flowers of all kinds. There is even a competition for the best blooming *patio*, and the tourist office gives out maps of those open to the public. I am a bit concerned that Misty might pee against a precious flowerpot or up a rare tree. She was the only girl in the litter and probably learnt to pee like a boy dog from her brothers, lifting a leg. This confuses many people who would stop in the street to enquire if my dog is a boy or a girl. Some even go to the length of demonstrating physically that the dog has just lifted its leg to pee rather than sat down, like a girl. Thankfully, body language is international; this is so handy when you don't understand a single word of amazed, rapidly babbling strangers, lifting one leg.

We walk on to find small craft shops where the tradition of making *cuero repujado* (embossed leather) has been kept for centuries as well as filigree silver jewellery and pottery. Cordoba is well-known, especially for the leather goods. Passing some restaurants, I see the typical Cordoban *gazpacho* on the menu. This is thick, fragrant, bright-red, cold soup with bits of boiled egg on the top, called '*salmorejo*'. Also on the menu are other local specialities such as '*rabo de toro*' (oxtail stew), or '*sopa de ajo*' with raisins. I actually cannot stand the fluffed-up sodden bread in garlic soup and quickly turn away. At another place, they have honeyed lamb and meats stuffed with dates and nuts. Although this is mouth-wateringly tempting and dogs are usually permitted to sit under the outdoor tables, we just do not have the money for such treats and move on, starving, to buy '*un pan*', a freshly baked bread.

Unlike Laurie, I have not seen any men wearing 'tall Cordobese hats, blue shirts, scarlet waistbands, and girls with smouldering Arab faces', but instead I see groups of Japanese girls posing and taking pictures of each other whilst constantly giggling.

Gripped by a mad impulse, I feel like turning off the A4/E5 to go to 'Ladronera', just because the name appeals to me, meaning either 'female thief' or 'stolen stash'. On second thoughts, I realize that it is not a place at all but the name of a mountain and I must not digress to go treasure hunting by tall mountains.

Just then the mileage clocks 0000, and I have done the

first thousand miles since starting this trip. The heat is rising, and I am driving along the '*autovía*' in my black bra and knickers, eating the loaf, biting bits of off the stick of bread. Lorry drivers seem to find this most amusing and toot their loud horns enthusiastically as I overtake them. I have to constantly wipe my face and neck with a small white facecloth, sweat pouring off me in regular showers. Somewhere after Andujar, I follow signs for a supermarket to buy tomatoes. I park in the shade and put my clothes back on. Guess what, there is a sign on the automatic doors saying '*Cerrado,15 de Mayo*'(closed, 15th of May) which is today. People wander in and out of the almost empty car park, peering through the locked doors, making quite sure the place really is closed. They assemble in small groups to discuss the situation.

'The doors are closed,' says one person to the other.

The other person goes, 'Closed?'

'The supermarket cannot be closed,' says third person.

A new arrival has just read the notice, saying, 'It says it is closed on the 15th.' They all check the date on their watches and mobiles. It is the 15th of May.

'Supermarkets can't be closed on Mondays,' says a newcomer. 'They have to open on Mondays.'

'Not this one,' replies the other person. 'Look, there is a sign on the door.'

'A sign on the door?' So it goes on and on; some people go off to discuss the situation more, others have a quick rest in their cars, all doors open, listening to loud melancholic flamenco tunes on the radio.

I have found the orange I bought in Alhama. It is the size of Misty's head. Hurray, food! Laurie found the pangs of hunger 'voluptuous'. I am just plain starving.

Luncheon over, I go onwards to Valdepeñas through Castilla - La Mancha.

'There is no camping at Valdepeñas,' three old men assure me, laughing, 'because all the land has been sold to build more houses!' They almost bend double with the fun of it all. I don't really fancy going wine tasting in some of the numerous *bodegas*. In this heat, alcohol is the last thing I need. Indeed nothing grabs my attention at all. Laurie says, the place felt rich with wide streets, and 'an air of privileged well-being, like an oil-well in a desert of hardship'. He was invited to play in a small brothel here, but I am getting back on the road.

However I am not going back to Santa Elena where I saw the last camping sign near the 'Desfiladero de Despenadoperros' (Narrow pass of the dogs that went over the cliff) and the nearby nature reserve of the same name. I don't want Misty to fall off a cliff, and I have been through ten tunnels up to now, my personal nightmare, and anyway, there's no going back.

I am driving through Castilla - La Mancha. 'La Mancha' is Arabic meaning dry, waterless land. This is exactly what it is. The vast plains are apparently unique in western Europe and remind some people of rural Australia or expanses of empty land in south-west America. I have never been there, so I don't know. I am driving along the '*ruta de Don Quixote*' as countless signs keep telling me. White paper posters seemingly drawn in pencil, showing Don Quixote and Sancho Panza, line the long, deserted road stretching out in front of me.

Here or there are ruins of windmills standing on small hills reminding me of the battle Don Quixote had with the white-sailed windmills, thinking they were outlaws, and Sancho going, 'No, man, they are just windmills...' I regard Don Quixote in a different light now, not seeing him as a freaky nutter madman but instead as someone perhaps suffering from mental derangement yet he surely chose his lifestyle, a choice between reality and imagination. It was here in La Mancha where Sancho got so fed up with him, he even planned on leaving him to it, sneaking off secretly to leave Don Quixote to his 'madness'. He could take no more. But surely he must have been a bit 'mad' himself going off with him in the first place? I feel one could go mad in this desert without any help at all. The place is completely deserted. Don Quixote did meet a real duke and duchess and lived in a real palace where he was totally accepted as a real knight-errant. Sancho's dream came true and he got to rule over an island. But the responsibility of government weighed him down. He got depressed and was on his way back to the palace when he fell into a great big hole in the ground, giving him the opportunity to think of ambitions as being totally futile. You see, dear reader, I am beginning to crack the Cervantes code. Dressing Don Quixote up in 'madness' was only a code to take the mickey out of the lifestyles portrayed by knight-errants in romantic novels. Don Quixote himself fell asleep and woke up into sanity. The people around him were grief-stricken and unable to cope with this new Don Quixote; they liked the mad, old freak. However, it can't have been all bad since, as Cervantes put it, 'after all the niece continued to eat, the housekeeper drank, and washed down sorrow, and Sancho Panza made much of himself: for there is a strange charm in the thoughts of a good legacy, or the hopes of an estate, which wondrously removes, or at least alleviates, the sorrow that men would otherwise feel for the death of friends'.

Here we are now coming into Ciudad Real. There is a museum 'del Quixote' here with loads of old copies of 'Don Quixote', some in Esperanto and Braille. As for the town, I had thought it would be something to do with '*Real*', royal, maybe a nice old palace thrown in here or there. The only things I see are thrown-together piles of ugly houses. Don't go there if you don't have to. You haven't missed a thing. The only thing I like about this place is a guy wearing a black T-shirt with the letters FBI on the front.

On the way out, I pass a dirty-looking sugar refinery.

The red earth of the Sierra Morena is now covered in ripe corn and green vines. How did Laurie walk all this way? He has Ciudad Real on his map but does not make one mention of it. I am not surprised. And he got a lift from a farmer on the way into Valdepeñas, 'exclaiming that no stranger should walk while he rode, and proudly answered my gift of a cigarette by giving me in exchange a miniature cucumber'.

Laurie would just sleep in a ditch by the road and I am now looking at ditches appearing 'sleepable'. Red ditches. Here now are bright green trees, but the shadows are getting longer. In the village of Orgaz, I spot a small '*hostal*' and I am sorely tempted to call it a day. But no, on to Toledo.

The town looks fabulous at night and is beautifully lit up. I take the wrong turn of course and end up in a dead-end road by a church somewhere where I don't want to be. I feel exactly like Laurie. 'I felt once again the unease of arriving at night in an unknown city - that faint sour panic which seems to cling to a place until one has found oneself a bed', or in my case, a campsite which permitted dogs. On the verge of panicking, lost in a strange town, I finally spot a camping sign, and here is 'El Greco', the campsite. Phew. It is not cheap at sixteen euros per night, but dogs are allowed. There is even toilet paper in the washrooms, but the toilet-brush holders are nailed to the floor. I wonder what that's all about.

The plots for campers are neatly hedged. The tent is up within minutes and the tea brewed. Over dinner, yes a tomatoe and the other half of the jar of beans, I notice German caravanners next door putting up a satellite dish as soon as they arrive. Then the table comes out, and a TV is placed on it. Out come two chairs. The guy tells me how he was worried sick earlier, driving along at top speed when he noticed that the clutch pedal had got stuck somehow. The wife had to do the steering as he dived under the dashboard, groping around the clutch pedal.

'*Was ist denn das?*'(Whatever is that?), he thought, ripping at half a sandal, stuck under the pedal. With one final pull he freed up the pedal, and dived back up, taking over the wheel once more after handing his wife his mashed-up sandal.

'*Ja, und wo ist die andere Hälfte?*'(OK but where is the other half?) she asked, then dived under dash herself till the other half of the sandal was discovered. What if it had got under the brake! It was stuck in the door.

'*Da kann man mal sehen, warum man nicht in Sandalen fahren soll. Tja.*'(You find out why you should not drive wearing sandals), the German bloke laughs. Not a man with sensitive feet then, I guess, because, surely you would notice driving with one shoe on and one shoe off, I am thinking as I take Misty for a little walk to the posh-looking bar, to read maps and drink beer. Soon the lack of light or the beer kicking in make reading impossible. The biters are out and I need to find the lemon oil. Exhausted, I drag myself back to the tent.

16 May 2006

Laurie dragged himself into town, staggeringly, and then collapsed in a shop. Men carried him over to a water-trough, laying him down to cool off. Walking through the August heat had been too much. Old women sitting nearby were tutting about his head and how he had no hat, 'sad fool'. He woke up in the middle of the night to a 'cold white moon' and discovered that someone had covered him with a sack. By morning, he was miraculously recovered, and I reckon one of the old crones must have slipped him a dose of homeopathic belladonna to cure him.

On the campsite, the Dutch have been faffing since 7 am. I eventually get up at 8 am, by which time the Dutch have nearly stopped, but then the Germans start. Now it's the Japanese-looking people. All three of them have funny walks; one seems to be on tiptoes, the other does a sort of continuous hop, skip and jump, the third walks like a John Wayne-type who has lost his horse. Between them they go backwards and forwards with endless stuff to be washed or toileted. Now a couple and a kid emerge from the same tent. Wow, how many people have slept in that, it's not a big tent! The Dutch caravan is moving on its own to align itself, perfectly radio-controlled, to the tow bar of the car. The Japanese lookalikes look on, transfixed. The Dutch couple are speaking in their clipped English. The Japanese go 'Ah' and 'Eh' and 'Hem' and 'Hmnoi'. An English-looking man walks by with bread under his arm, saying nothing at all. The German couple have got their TV going. I plan to pack up and leave after a shower. Caravanners are not really me, and I am surrounded by them, clicking plastic here, hooking something there, folding or unfolding tables and chairs, and cleaning constantly; it's all a world of funny new noises that fat flocks of sparrows are frantically trying to cover up.

Over the luxury of a second cup of tea, half of a still warm baguette from the site's shop and the obligatory tin of sardines, I listen to the Germans. They say a bus goes to the Old Town every hour and how Toledo is the most beautiful city in all of Spain. Oh no, I can smell German coffee, so I quickly tie the dog on the long washing line lead under a shaded tree, and leave her with her water bowl to guard the car, and perhaps do a bit of sparrow watching.

At the bus stop everybody is in couples, speaking four or six different languages, only to each other. I feel like a lone wolf in married couple country. This is going to be a long wait. I sit myself on the pavement, thinking about the huge flowerpots, placed at the cornerescorners of some fields in La Mancha. What are these things for - jugs the height of two grown men standing on top of each other - water, sunflower oil, what? Advertisements for '*Se vende*' (for sale) painted on thetheir big terracotta bellies - the land, the jug or what? I am too shy to ask around, and guess that the couples might feel my questions a little intrusive.

On the way into town, uphill, I am glad that I am not walking and I see two nuns getting on the bus. One is all in black, the other in white. Veiled, with crosses on their chests, and the ring on their finger, they are married, as my mum would say, 'to God'. Handbags, sensible footwear and all, I wonder if they are tourists, or maybe teachers.

The city of three cultures, '*la ciudad de la tres culturas*', is where Muslims, Christians and Jews lived together in harmony. Apparently. Till Felipe II took over from Carlos I and took any royal business away from the Catholic church to Madrid.

I am unsure as to all the harmony of the three cultures living together thing. After all, there is the 'Bitter Well' or '*Pozo Amargo*' in the centre of the medieval district south of the cathedral. At this well a young Jewish woman cried heart-wrenching tears every day, turning the water bitter forever, after her father killed her Christian lover. In 1492, all Jews were kicked out of town unless they converted to Catholicism, as decreed by Isabel and Fernando.

I am standing in the Plaza de Zocodover, locally known as 'Zoco', where Laurie set himself up to play to the open-air cafés. One evening, a special family party arrived and seated themselves 'as though in a box at the opera'. As Laurie went around for the collection, the woman of the party turned out to be English and invited Laurie to join them. A man with the 'eyes of a burnt-out eagle' introduced himself. 'Roy Campbell,' he said. 'South African poet. Er - reasonably well-known in your country.'

Laurie stayed with the family for over a week, sleeping in a bed held up at one end by a pile of books. 'Roy drank four and a half litres of wine a day, he said' is Laurie's description of Roy, a formidable character who found 'consolations of living in Toledo' in wine and El Greco.

'Never seen him? You must. Bloody marvellous, boy. Wake me up tomorrow and I'll take you round,' said Roy.

They started with the 'Annunciation' and Roy explained what the painting meant to him, 'with a kind of groping reverence'.

'A bloody miracle, that hand. And look at that light in the sky. Pure Toledo - only he was the first bugger to see it.'

They went further up into town to see El Greco's house, now the 'Casa-Museo de El Greco', then 'a shaggy intimate little villa, full of dead flowers and idiot guides. Inside were the paintings; colours I'd never seen before, weeping purples, lime greens, bitter yellows; the long skulls of the saints and their sunken eyelids, eyes coated with ecstatic denials, limbs and faces drawn upwards like spires ascending, robes flickering like tapered flames...'. But El Greco exhausted them both and soon they were off to the bars.

El Greco came to Toledo in 1577 but failed to get the job of court artist with Felipe II. Yet he managed to build a client base of rich fans and enjoyed living life in the fast lane. At one point he was even taken to court by the cathedral administrators for charging outrageously high prices for his works! The painting of 'The Burial of the Count of Orgaz' shows how St Stephen and St Augustine descended from heaven to miraculously attend the burial. Amongst the bystanders, El Greco painted himself, his son, and, wait for it, Cervantes.

Today's Toledo reminds me of Edinburgh's Old Town, with countless cobblestoned alleyways and tall old buildings. The tourist shops are stacked with steel jewellery. Steel of incredible purity is produced here and manufactured into anything from swords and knives, full knightsknight's armour and bracelets and trinkets to fancy rings and brooches often encrusted with black, jet-like stones, or the steel blackened with a background of fine gold or silver patterns on plates and pictures. I buy a postcard showing two men and a baby. The painting is called 'The Bearded Woman' by Ribera, and it shows a grim-looking old man offering his one swollen breast to the baby in his arms. He is wearing a long gown. Behind him is a man dressed in black, looking extremely worried. Or maybe he is just constipated.

Here now is a bakery shop, its huge window display is a teenager-height sculpture of the cathedral which is entirely made of baked marzipan. I dive into the shop and buy two small bits of this delicacy, one dusted with powdered chocolate, the other covered in pine nuts. Two euros, oof, but what a melt-in-the-mouth sugar-hit food experience!

Then I realize I have missed the bus. Waiting outside the pensioner's club I watch coaches roll by full of tourists, then busloads of screaming school kids roaming the streets and narrow avenues. A stranger asks me for a light. A crane is working overhead. I love watching cranes. A workman high up on the building site waves a brick in the air, shouting down, '*guapa*' (gorgeous), which sounds like 'whopper'. Another bloke arrives on a bicycle, expertly jamming its pedal on the kerbside, to watch me waiting. I have a cigarette, reading posters of

Sting coming into town, and trendy DJs playing later in May. I am beginning to stress out a bit; there is still no bus. Buses, yes, lots of them come and go, but none go in the direction of the campsite. Finally, my bus stutters and wheezes around the corner. I am the only passenger. I tell the driver that I am late for the campsite, and I am worried that they might charge me double. At least that is what I think I am saying. Well, the driver puts his foot down and screeches around the town like a man possessed, driving the bus downhill like an ambulance out on a call.

I race back, collect the dog and the car and turn up hot and breathless at the solid, wooden office hut. I explain to the pockmarked-faced man that I got lost in Toledo and missed the bus. This is what I hope I say, in my rubbish Spanish. He grins coolly, hands me my passport, does not charge me extra and goes, '*de nada*' (it's nothing).

Back on the road, Misty and I are heading in the direction of Madrid. Laurie was 'given a lift by two racy young booksellers...very gay' who pointed out all the brothels as they got into town. Madrid is the highest capital in Europe, and the temperature is nearing forty degrees in the shade, says the man on the radio. I guess I could take Misty to the 'Parque de Buen Retiro', sometimes referred to as the 'green lungs' of the city, just around the corner from the Prado. This park has an outdoor gym for retired people which apparently is a favourite with the elderly, doing enthusiastic workouts here. Then again, Misty and I could go to the Parque del Oeste in the hope of spying out some transsexual prostitutes; now that could be entertaining. I quite fancy the Casa de Campo, not just to go prostitute-spotting but to imagine wild bears roaming in the semi-wilderness.

Madrid's coat of arms was originally very straightforward, merely saying, ' I was built on water and my walls are of fire'. Today, the numerous little rivers running under the city are all covered up, but the old town walls remain glittery flintstone. The emblem of Madrid was later enriched with the picture of a she-bear, eating from a *madroño* tree. This tree got its name from its fruit which looks like a strawberry. The picture is framed by seven five-point stars. There are various explanations. The one I like the best tells of the North Star and the constellation of seven stars near to it called Ursa Minor, small she-bear. In medieval times, bears were rambling and roving around the north of Madrid. Also, it is said that after Carlos I cured a fever with the leaves of the *madroño* tree, he gave permission for a picture of the imperial crown to be at the top of the coat of arms.

Laurie had a hunch that he could make some money in Madrid and went off to the town hall to get a licence to play his fiddle in the streets. He was sent from pillar to post, and went to the police station, only to end up at the Department of Agriculture. The officers were all very friendly and rolled him lots of cigarettes but could not find the right bit of paper. In the end, Laurie was told not to worry about any licence and just go ahead with his playing. He found a room at an inn, where the clock in the courtyard went mad, a few nights after his arrival, striking fourteen.

'It hasn't struck for years,' said the innkeeper and went off to 'hit it with a bottle'.

Laurie's bedroom was 'a cell without windows, and had bedbugs as big as beetles. Lying down was to be ridden, racked and eaten, to scratch and fight for breath. It was clear why everyone stayed awake in this city. Only in the streets and courtyards could one breathe at night, and the heat brought the beds alive'. I would have died on the spot. Only this morning, a large black beetle, seemingly without a head, had crawled across my face and I nearly died from shock.

Some say the best time to visit Madrid is in August, when the hectic city life is holidaying on the beaches and the place is almost empty with temperatures soaring to well over forty-three degrees in the shade. However, it is a dry heat and apparently the nights are cooler and pleasant due to the breezes flowing down from the sierras. I don't feel like being caught in city chaos although there are many soothing spas here, some with pools full of lemons! Now that sounds tempting, but what to do with the dog? I have also heard of a small Arab Spa with hot, warm or freezing pools which is joined to a Moroccan restaurant, the entire place smelling heavenly due to the heavily scented oils used for massage treatments.

Laurie found himself a manager, Concha, a 'husky young widow', who did his marketing for a small share in the profits. She had yellow hair, looking like 'a load of straw' which she conditioned with fish oil. Laurie fancied her something rotten but being slightly older than him, 'in her ripe middle twenties', he felt she was out of his reach. Yet one morning, he noticed her 'hot lazy eyes wandering' over him.

'My clothes, she said, were without class or dignity and not proper for an Englishman. What I needed, at least, was a pair of trousers, and she said she'd get some from a gentleman she knew. "You will have them tonight, I promise you. Then you will be able to walk in the street with honour"'.

On his last night in town, Laurie went for a pub crawl after finishing busking. Still unused to the heavy wine, he went from place to place and got completely blitzed. 'I was suddenly aware of the beauty of my fingernail'; oh dear, oh dear, here we go. Yet through the shreds of conversations he makes his readers aware, for the first time, of the stewing brew of European politics. He had mentioned his girlfriend's father in London, talking of the theory of anarchy, the necessity of political and personal freedom and his contempt for moral law. Laurie himself had even gone on strike in solidarity with his co-workers on a building site when some non-union members had been smuggled onto the site by the managers. The strike lasted two weeks. There was no revolution, just two weeks 'of hunger'. Also, Laurie had referred to spotting mysterious graffiti and the picture of Marx in a shop window on his arrival in Vigo. This was 1935. My German mother would have been all of thirteen with Hitler already powering ahead. Once a week, she would have to attend the Hitler Youth club where women instructed the girls on subjects now long forgotten but probably of a political nature. My mother tells me that it seemed ridiculous teaching politics to ten-year-olds. She recalls, that they had to learn '*Antreten*', standing in rows of three, behind a woman carrying a staff topped with a little flag. The girls all had to wear a uniform: a blue skirt with two pockets, a white blouse, a triangular black scarf tied at the neck with a leather ring, white knee-socks, black shoes, and a '*Kletterjacke*' (Climbing Jacket), brown, with four pockets made from '*Affenstoff*' (Monkey material) as they called fake suede at the time. The uniforms were expensive, and she had to ask for one for her birthday as one was not allowed to turn up in just any old cardigan. However, there were no travel restrictions for women in Germany unlike in Franco's Spain where women had to have the permission of their husbands to travel anywhere at all and divorce was illegal. I, for one, would have been completely snookered. But let's return to that bar in Madrid, seventy years ago. Laurie was about to fall in love with a gypsy waif behind the bar, and he was just imagining her naked feet when a minor bullfighter and his friends walked in. It was time to leave.

'I walked back through the streets with a rocking head, thinking simple ironic thoughts', he tells us. Dear reader, have you ever indulged in excessive alcohol consumption? I for one can imagine exactly what state Laurie was in. I am glad that the door was open as Laurie got back to the inn, cats darting 'across the yard like lizards'.

Even today, they say the night life in Madrid is second to none,

'As I stumbled upstairs a hand touched mine in the darkness and drew me into a jumbled moonlit room. "I've got your clothes," said Concha. She stood close against me, holding my shoulder blades, and I could smell her peppery flesh. "Man," she whispered. I swayed on my feet, full of hazy, unthinking dumbness. Somewhere in the room a child called "Mama", and the woman paused to give it a spoonful of jam. Then she took off my boots and helped me to bed. Before she joined me she made the sign of the cross'.

I bet it hasn't changed a bit.

Just a short way west out of Madrid is Alcalá de Henares, the birthplace of Cervantes, but I am rigidly sticking to Laurie's route, heading more across 'the immense plain of La Mancha, stretching flat as a cowhide' towards the Sierra de Guadarrama. At first, the road to Segovia is awful with four lines of heavy traffic, all going into the same direction, following signs of '*todas direcciones*' (all directions), and another four packed lanes of traffic going back towards Madrid. Coaches are wheezing along, lorries are puffing and motorbikes are roaring by, then tunnel number eleven and I've had it! This is not what I had in mind. The giraffe is looking at me with some concern. I recognize my symptoms of tea shortage. This needs to be dealt with. Soon enough, there is a sign for La Coruña, which is a place hundreds of miles north of here, but I chance it and turn off the motorway to a national road. What a relief. I have found the A6, hopefully leading eventually to Segovia.

Up we go now along the narrow winding road, up and up. Some lorries have given up the climb temporarily and are parked in the passing places. We go on up and round and up the south face of the mountain, 'a raw burnt rock, the cliffs stripped bare by the sun'. Laurie climbed to the six thousand feet pass of Puerto de Navacerrado after taking a shower in a waterfall; brrrh, that must have been freezing. He says that he 'was never so alive and so alone again'. I really sympathize with Laurie on the 'alone' bit. At one point on his travels, Laurie was joined by a young man who soon got on his nerves.

'No longer could I imagine myself prince of the road, the lone ranger my fancy preferred. I'd developed an ingrowing taste for the vanity of solitude...' I know how you felt, Laurie.

But something else occurred to him in the Sierra de Guadarrama: 'Crossing the Sierra was not just a stage on my journey, in spite of the physical barrier. It was also one of those sudden, jerky advances in life, which once made closes the past for ever. It was a frontier in more ways than one, and not till I'd passed it did I feel really involved in Spain'.

I park the car in the dense forest of ancient pine trees before the descent. Huge boulders are lying around covered in moss and little blue flowers, with beams of hazy sunlight pointing through the treetops. After some wild peeing and stick throwing and a cup of lukewarm tea from the thermos, Misty and I are off down through more cool green forests of the north face. Down and round and down we go, eventually arriving at a vast stretch of plain flat countryside.

I fire up the stove and put the kettle on and get out the yellow plastic chair, to sit under a tree and survey the scene. There's a '*hacienda*' type farmhouse surrounded by cypresses in the distance, flat farmland shimmering with heat, stretching out for miles around, a forest behind me. I pick some raspberries, pee in the ditch and get back on the way.

Within minutes, well, less than half an hour, the dog and I approach the outskirts of Segovia. The streets are deserted, siesta time; between 2 pm and 5 pm, Spain eats, sleeps, makes love or dreams somewhere in the shade. Some little information kiosk is closed. Where to camp? A gypsy-looking girl in jeans is walking near a bus stop as if the heavy heat did not exist. I pull in, get out of the car and ask her, my face beetroot with the heat, 'Is there any camping nearby?' Totally unfazed, the girl goes, '*¡Tranquila!*' (Chill out), and explains how to get there.

Her arms are waving and pointing through the air into definite directions. I don't understand a word she says and imagine a 'like the crow flies' path to the campsite, '*muy cerca, es facil*' (very near, it's easy), are the last words I get. What eyes, what sparkle of composed confident '*independencia*'(independence), what air of freedom mixed with grace. Wow! As if hypnotised, I get back into the car, make a perfect U-turn and head directly into the campsite, truly, within minutes.

There is nobody there. Oh, fluff. What if the place is closed?

Dense forest is on my left. Then there is suddenly a wooden cabin bearing the sign '*oficina*'. I stop the car and take a look around. There are wooden toilet huts, painted in gay flaking whites and reds, a small bar, wooden shutters, closed. A man appears from somewhere. He opens the office hut and takes in my German passport, English car, and dog in the back.

'*¿Una noche?*'(One night?) he enquires. I pay cash and he tells me to pitch my tent anywhere I like.

But for two caravans, the place is deserted. It used to be a field, the camping spots are merely marked out with lines of large, white stones. In the vicinity of some other toilet block, toilets are very important to me, I park and set up the tent near some handy table-and-benches-nailed-together thing.

'CUP OF TEA!' roars my mind. Misty pees up against a tree. I have the kettle on the stove on the table, very laid-back luxury.

The late afternoon unfolds into early evening as I stare at snow-capped majestic mountains in the distance. Now, the snowy crags of the Guadarrama are covered by a perfect circle of orange evening sunlight. I have the other half of the baguette and a small tin of tuna with lots of pepper.

If this goes on for much longer i may go out of my mind she is feeding breadcrumbs to the sparrows you know watching them intently trying to hear what they are thinking oh no 8 pm i cannot believe i am still tied to a tree and she has the horrible lemon oil stuff now smearing it over her burnt face yep the biters are out and even the crickets sounding like when she lights the stove very frightening like a firework about to go off the cricket chorus is moving in closer but dog sparrows of all shapes and sizes are fluttering sexy spring flirtations around the place a girl came earlier to look at me shading under the table picking up a crumb of bread then six of them or maybe four i cannot count that well fluttered by ate and left here is one boy now stretching his neck to take us in more dog and all i have to eat is multi-coloured dog biscuits and empty tuna fish tins to lick out with flies in my water bowl one more of these boring offensive meals and i will chew through that long lead and find myself some real chorizo

Misty is throwing very disapproving looks at me. I guess she is desperate for the toilet so I grab a plastic bag and take her for a short walk, off the lead. The sparrows have almost finished the breadcrumbs I sprinkled into the grass earlier. A small girl sparrow hops in to try her luck at the leftovers but a boy immediately flies in to shout her off. She cocks her head marked with the elegant creamy-coloured eye stripe, hops to the side, and gently waits. A stork suddenly flies almost directly over my head with a lump of food in its beak. Overhead is a vast funnel-shaped cloud.

Like Laurie, I feel 'fat with time' once more, at last totally relaxed in the peaceful surroundings.

As it is too dark to read, I decide to have a 'foot event'. Sitting cross-legged in the tent, my hands inspect my feet to deal with any stuck-on bits, dole out arnica cream to sore and rough patches, scratch and dig unashamedly under the toenails. There is no doubt about it in my mind; my feet are definitely the most adorable part of my entire body. Filing and clipping away merrily, I am joined by Mr Whyte and Mr Mackay join me, the whisky people, for the evening, and together we mellow out in the dark till it is time to sleep. I have just blown out the candle when I notice a man with a torch approaching the tent.

'*¡Señora!*' he shouts. '*¡Peligro! ¡Peligro! ¡Hay un lobo en el bosque, cuídate, es muy peligroso!*' (Lady! Danger! Danger! There is a wolf in the forest, take care, it is very dangerous!) He is flapping his arms madly, pointing at the open tent door so I will close it. He shines the his torch into my face and then at the far-off forest where I see a group of men with long sticks and fiery torches shouting and beating at the undergrowth. I take one look around the tent, my heart sinking. There is no dog.

'*¡Hombre, no es un lobo peligroso, no, es mi perro!*' (Man, that's not a dangerous wolf, it's my dog!) I reply, taking in a deep breath and bellowing across the entire campsite, 'Misteeeh!' twice, at top volume. The man tells me off for yelling so loudly, people are asleep. Within moments there is a rustle, and here is Misty Blue, her eyes mad with wild panic, her tongue hanging down to her feet sideways, her coat wet with mud, bits of branch sticking from it. The man cannot believe his eyes. I tell him, that this is my dog, not a wolf. He is visibly vexed and tells me in no uncertain terms to get out of the campsite. I say I will, in the morning. Dead right. II shall leave tomorrow. Wolf, my foot. I go to sleep with the dog's lead tied around my ankle, like the man with a goat tethered to his leg in Laurie's story.

Embarrassed to their bones, Whyte and Mackay have slunk off into the dark.

17 May 2006

We slink off like thieves at first light. What a night!

Segovia is deserted at this early hour and parking is easy. Misty and I walk to check out the aqueduct. Its arches are breathtakingly high. Laurie watched a movie here projected from some window onto a huge white canvas spread between one of the aqueduct's gigantic arches. I wonder which window and cannot find the arch that had been converted into a bar during Laurie's time. Maybe they closed it down as the town was declared a World Heritage City by UNESCO in 1975, a ridge-top town at 1002 metres above sea level with two rivers at its base. We climb to the top, and a man approaches, asking if I am American.

'Certainly not,' I reply and stalk off in my kitten heels. He had just interrupted my vision of someone driving along the top of the aqueduct. Today I am in my black and white kittenheel sandals, the badly fitting cut-off jeans, a sleeveless black and white stripey jumper and a thin black cardigan with a very wide neckline, exposing bits of burnt shoulders. Starving, I walk into a cake shop. The lady shopkeeper in her frilly crisp-white apron is superfriendly. I buy a mouth-watering '*pastel*', flaky pastry thing with baked apple (*manzana*) and custard (*crema*) inside, and some bread. This is stuffed into my small backpack, whilst the cake gets the cardboard treatment. It is formally laid out onto a small paper tray, then a strip of card is bent around it to prevent the wrapping paper touching the delicacy. The friendly lady wishes me '*Buen viaje*' (Safe journey) as I balance the treasure on the palm of my hand, untying the dog's lead with the other. Off we go now, me hobbling precariously over the cobblestones of the narrow streets, to stare at the cathedral and on to find the Alcazar. It has the distinctive features of Rapunzel's towers, the turrets are topped with slate 'witches' hats', and there is a really deep moat. The Romans fortified the original Arab castle, ('*al-qasr*') and in the thirteenth and fourteenth centuries it was expanded even further. However, the whole thing burnt down in 1862 but was entirely reconstructed to the OTT glory of today. It is said that Walt Disney was inspired by its fairytale design and used it as a model for Sleeping Beauty's castle in Disneyland.

As we walk back into the narrow old streets, I suddenly feel as if I have lived here before, in a previous life, studying music. The place is humming with harmonies. Then I come across a small marketplace amongst the alleyways, and here is the most beautiful sight: a group of around two hundred seven- or nine-year-olds are sitting on some steps as if in some impromptu amphitheatre, watching a medieval puppet show - real medieval puppets, actors in medieval clothes playing medieval instruments, telling stories of the past. The children are enchanted and fascinated, their eyes huge, some with their mouths open, they sit, staring at the spectacle. One small boy has folded a lady's fan from a blank sheet of paper and keeps putting it on top of his head as if it is a precious tortoiseshell comb holding a delicate lace mantilla in place. A teacher signals for him to stop but he takes no notice at all.

I have unwrapped the cake and sink my teeth into the sweet apple and custard pastry.

Laurie says, 'Segovia was a city in a valley of stones - a compact, half forgotten heap of architectural splendours built for the glory of some other time. I liked the snug city which seemed to ignore the invention of the wheel, where naked children darted into their tattered houses like pheasants into nests of bracken.'

But, like me, he was blown away by the aqueduct: 'The Roman aqueduct came looping from the hills in a series of arches, some rising to over a hundred feet, and composed of blocks of granite weighing several tons and held together by their weight alone. This imperial gesture, built to carry water from a spring ten miles away, still strode across the valley with massive grace, a hundred vistas framed by its soaring arches, to enter the city at last, high above the rooftops, stepping like a mammoth among the houses. "The Aqueduct," said the farmer, who had given Laurie a lift into town on his mule cart, in case he might not have noticed it.

'"It's like a bridge," he went on. "You could drive across it with a coach and horses."

'"Wouldn't it be too narrow?" I asked.

'He looked at me sharply.

'"I drove across it in a narrow coach."'

I have lost the car. In a rising panic I notice all the parked cars have stickers on them, their parking paid for. I had no idea about this. What if they have towed the car away and I'll have to spend the rest of the day trying to find the police car pound and pay vast amounts of euros for the fine?

this is like when she lost the car before i know fine it is only up the road but does anybody listen to me

Here it is now, phew. But what's this? I have a pink parking ticket. Dear reader, I confess I threw the paper away, ignoring it completely. Laurie went to La Granja on his way south where Felipe V built a copy of Versailles, his grandfather's place (Louis XIV), in San Ildefonso, twelve kilometres east of Segovia. The twenty-eight fountains were magically switched on when Laurie spent an hour there, totally alone except for some aged gardeners. Laurie felt the gardens were like a wind-up 'monarch's toy, of which the owner had rapidly tired...La Granja...was more than a little vulgar - a royal inflation of a suburban mind'. I decide not to go there. I want to get some distance behind me, burn more rubber. So I focus on Valladolid on the map.

I leave town, passing 'suicide rock' or what looks like it. Here, a beautiful Jewess accused of adultery was cast from the rock, but 'she called on the Virgin to prove her innocence, and was compassionately halted while still in mid-air and allowed to float to the ground'. The massive rock above the little church is circled by huge raptors as I take the road to my next destination.

I can feel the mind going. It is off on a right regular rant, systematically building bundles of prejudices against the place of Valladolid. It was here that Isabel and Fernando got married on the quiet, only to team up with Torquemada, the Father of the Inquisition idea, to kill or torture, or both, anyone non-Christian. Torquemada, himself a Jew and born in Valladolid, was totally disguised in his job as a Catholic priest and also became Isabel's private confessor. So he really had it made. Four years later, he was appointed by the Pope Sixtus IV as the leader of the Castilian Inquisition. The eight hundred year struggle to rid Spain of non-Christians now focused on Jews. Spain had the largest population of Jews in medieval Europe and there had been many conversions and intermarriages, so it was difficult to establish who exactly had 'sangre limpia' (clean blood), and who did not. However, Torquemada thought up some guidelines for rooting out heretics, but especially Jews: if you cleaned your house on Friday night and lit candles early, you were a Jew; if you ate unleavened bread and started your meal with lettuce and celery during Holy Week, you were a Jew; if you were praying facing a wall and leaning forwards and backwards, you were a Jew.

Once pronounced Jewish, your property would be seized, providing a handy income to further the means of the Reconquista against the Muslims. Then you would be marched through the streets wearing a short yellow shirt patterned with crosses ('sambenito'), your genitals exposed, before you got flogged in front of the church. But if you were in real trouble, torture awaited you and a burning at the stake. If you repented, you would be burnt quickly with dry wood. If not, you would be burnt above a stake of sodden damp wood, increasing your agony. More than two thousand Jews were murdered in the 1480s by the Inquisition. At one point, eight Jews were convicted of having sacrificed a Christian child, and although no victim was ever found or body identified, the Jews were killed. Torquemada used this to try to persuade Isabel and Fernando to expel all Jews from Spain. However, they were offered thirty thousand ducats by two rich Jews, and they needed money badly. Torque-mada is said to have told them, 'Judas sold Christ for thirty pieces of silver, and you would sell Him for thirty thousand.' He had no wish to be involved any further. In 1492, he achieved his ambition when Isabel and Fernando decreed all Jews should leave the country.

In the same year, they also gave Columbus the go-ahead with his plan to discover Asia. I think Columbus had read the book by Marco Polo who had travelled to Asia with his father and uncle two hundred years before. They had reached China and served at the Court of Kublai Khan. Marco Polo had not just brought back the idea of spaghetti from his travels which lasted fifteen years. He wrote of the countless riches of the East. Still strapped for cash, it must have been this which persuaded Isabel and Fernando to sponsor an expedition for Columbus to sail west across the Atlantic and return laden with treasures. He, in my opinion, had a totally different idea: he wanted to prove that the world was not flat but, in fact, round. Had he so much as mentioned this plan to the royal couple, they would surely never have agreed to such a plan as they were staunch supporters of the Catholic Church in whose interest it was to have people believe in a flat world. Questioning this alone would probably have made you an instant 'heretic' at the time. Maybe suspecting this 'crazy' and potentially 'heretical' notion, Italy or the Vatican had earlier declined any support of the entire mission. Furthermore, if Columbus wanted to discover Asia, then why did he not turn to his left or right which is the way to Asia?

I believe, at the time maps only showed longitudes, not latitudes, but how important is this when you own a compass and have brilliant navigation skills? I reckon he knew very well what he was doing, going directly west to hit the horizon and prove it is impossible to fall over the edge and off the world, which therefore had to be a round ball. He went with three small ships. His crew of one hundred and twenty men were on the brink of mutiny and gave Columbus just two more days after sailing for thirty-one days west of the Canary Islands. Then he found the first island and named it 'San Salvador' (Holy Saviour), not surprising in the circumstances. He then discovered Cuba and Hispaniola and returned a hero eight months later, to be congratulated by Isabel and Fernando. After this, he set off on three more expeditions and found Jamaica and Trinidad as well as other Caribbean islands and even got as far as the South American mainland and Mexico. He returned laden with treasure and brought incredible riches to Spain which extracted vast amounts of gold and silver from the new colonies over the centuries. At one point, Columbus was arrested because he had shown that he was a useless administrator and was taken back to Spain and released soon after. It is a bit like Sancho Panza in Cervantes' story of Don Quixote to my mind, but written almost a hundred years later. Columbus, incredibly, died poor and alone in Valladolid. Sure, there is the 'Casa Museo de Colon' (Columbus Museum), a replica of the house he lived and died in, but I cannot persuade myself to go, feeling his treatment was completely unacceptable. He was never rewarded for his brilliance and heroic determinism.

Seville became the trade monopoly with the new continent, and one of the richest places in Europe, all due to Columbus.

Cervantes was born forty-one years after Columbus died. Aged nineteen, he had to flee the country as he was being done for assault. He ended up with a permanently wounded arm from the Battle of Lepanto, then he got involved when Tunis was seized, after which he hopped back from Italy to Spain, only to be captured by pirates and sold as a slave in Algiers! It took him five years and four attempts before he finally got out. He then tried to go to America. It didn't work out. Instead, he became a tax collector in Granada but went to prison in Seville for seven months due to mismanagement of the accounts. He used this opportunity to write poems of sardonic comment on the contemporary politics. Then he got his girlfriend pregnant and finally got married to his wife. The illegitimate baby was raised in his family once they had moved to Valladolid in 1604. It was here that he wrote the first part of Don Quixote. It was also here in Valladolid that he was imprisoned for some incident but released soon after. Police records showed the address of his house as Calle Rastro 7 which, today, is open for visitors.

Present-day Valladolid is probably a thriving, rocking place with a vibrant university scene, but I'm not coming in to stay. Look what happened to Laurie here. On his last night he gets back to his inn, where the '*borracho*' (drunk) innkeeper had previously told him to go 'sleep in the river', only to find the front door ripped off by the hinges, splintered wood all across the stone floor. Then he sees his landlady standing in the dark inside, brandishing a spade,

'I will kill him!' she cried. 'He is bad - bad!'

'He comes home like a pig, and I lock him out. But he breaks down the door and tries to love Elvira - ELVIRA!' She turned suddenly and screamed out the name, beating the ground with the flat of the spade. (In Spain all spades are set at a ninety degree angle from the handle, imagine the sparks flying off that).

'Daughter! Daughter!' The spade rang like a bell. 'I will smash his *cojones* (balls) against his teeth!'

Overall, Laurie commented on Valladolid like this: 'There are certain places one leaves never expecting to see again and I don't ever wish to return to that city'.

I am stuck on the ring road around it. There are lots of direction signs but none for Zamora, my next destination. I have just gone round it for the second time. There are hundreds of rectangular containers the size of lorries lying about painted pink, pastel-blue, eggshell white, pale peppermint-green, buttery-yellow, all just lying around, higgledy-piggledy, pastel dirt stuck to them under the grey sky. I pull in at a petrol station to ask my way out. I feel like leaving the engine running, in such a hurry to get out. I don't, naturally.

A most lovely Spanish man meets me at the doorway of the office.

'No, thank you, petrol, no. But please tell me how to leave this round road. I want to go to Zamora, but there are no signs for it.' I breathily wave my map in the air, showing the purple felt-tip pen marked route; you can probably hear my Spanish coming through, thick and rough.

'Ah, gasolina, ¿no?' he asks, having to repeat what I said initially. He is a meaty, muscly sort of man, a bit

taller than me with black waves of hair, my kind of age. I spread the map out on the bonnet of the car. He leans over it with me as we go through the Spanish conversational ritual of repetition and assertion.

'*No gasolina, gracias, no.*' I kick it off.

'*Vale, de nada,*' he makes the 'nothing' gesture over his shoulder, '*pero quiere Salamanca, no Zamora.*' (OK, it's nothing, but you want Salamanca, not Zamora).

I know what I want, and it is not Salamanca. I insist on Zamora after a few more repetitions and assertions. Smelling my lipstick, the man warms heavily to the interruption of this grey day.

He strokes the purply marked route on my map lovingly with his fingertip, turning to me, saying, 'Salamanca. You want to go to Salamanca.'

Actually, at this exact moment I feel like going into the office with him, locking the door and having wild passionate sex but I just contain myself.

'But Salamanca is to the south, I want to go west,' I assert myself.

'Yes, south at first, then after some kilometres there are signs for Zamora, yes, west. Zamora,' he breathes dreamily, 'signs for Zamora, later, much later!' Now he is pointing at the map. 'This map,' he says, 'it is an old one.'

'So am I,' I nearly blurt out, but still containing myself, get back into the car, good girl Misty, no barking, and find the exit to Salamanca. It takes ages of trust and patience, but after a while I do spy out the sign for Zamora, *muy bien*, and turn off.

Tordesillas was next on Laurie's journey with tiny unfindable villages on the way. My map, 'it is an old one', covers all of Europe in large brushstrokes, not including the smaller places. Relieved to be going in the right direction at last, I recall how Laurie was busking in Valladolid, licence and all, when a policeman drew his gun at the audience shouting, 'Have you no shame?' as he felt not enough money was coming into the musician's cap. If people wanted to listen, he would make them pay.

Tordesillas is marked by the word 'sunstroke' on Laurie's map.

He had walked the long straight road from Toro, through 'the violent heat...one's blood dried up and all juices vanishes...I kept on walking ...because it seemed to be the only way to agitate the air around me. I began to forget what I was doing on the road at all; I walked on as though keeping a vow, till I was conscious only of the hot red dust grinding like pepper between my toes...by mid-morning I was in a state of developing madness...' He ended up at some place, probably in Tordesillas, asking for water. People were saying it would kill him to drink, better to just suck a lump of ice. Laurie told them where he had come from.

'A woman threw up her hands. "On foot? It is not to be thought of!" The gentlemen started an argument, spitting radishes at each other like furious exclamations. "If he's English, he's the first walking Englishman I've seen," said one. "They walk all over the place," said the other. "Up and down mountainsides. Round and round poles." "Yes, yes - but they do not walk in Spain."' After that, Laurie was 'driven like a corpse to Valladolid'.

Toro looked like 'dried blood on a rusty sword' to Laurie. It was here that he witnessed his first parade. In Spain there is a great passion for parades, 'processions', particularly during Holy Week. Sitting outside a café, a stranger talked him through it as they watched the goings-on. A ten-year-old girl, all decked out like a small bride, wearing white gloves, and a 'halo of flowers' on her head was accompanied 'by two large women in black'.

'"See her," said Billette (the stranger). "Another virgin for the Carmelites. We offer one up almost every day...We are a holy town, as you see...Our girls marry Christ from the cradle. Where do they go? Into the caverns of the Church. We shan't see this one again."'

There are lots of churches in town, some with amazing Romanesque features. I wouldn't mind trying to spot the fly on the Virgin's dress, but the Colegiata Santa María La Mayor which houses the painting, 'Virgen de la Mosca', is closed. Back on the road towards Zamora, I remember Laurie stopping off somewhere around here where he got his first taste of flamenco dancing. He was playing a 'woozy fandango' he had learnt in Zamora, when suddenly his landlady sprang to life.

'The old man danced as if his life was at stake. While the woman was suddenly transformed, her great lumpen body becoming a thing of controlled and savage power. Moving with majestic assurance, her head thrown back, her feet pawing the ground like an animal, she stamped and postured round her small hopping husband as if she would tread him into oblivion'.

Laurie, I think you were scared!

Soon enough Misty and I arrive in Zamora on its rocky hill, the river Douro crawling along the bottom. The old town has its castle and many churches. It looks hot and asleep. On my way out, I find a supermarket. Hurray! Misty had a drink of warm water and is guarding the car from her open window. I wipe my face with the little white cloth, check the eyeliner and lipstick, and find the trolley park. I am starving. This could be a mistake, hungry in a supermarket, I will want to buy everything. But too late now. I am cruising the aisles, taking tins of sardines and tuna off shelves, *gazpacho* buy-one-get-one-free, dog food, fresh milk, eggs, thick slices of fat bacon, red peppers, oranges, tomatoes, whisky, and water. I have cunningly observed a woman paying with her plastic and intend to do the same. What's my number again, then it is back out into the sweltering heat. I drink a whole litre of cold *gazpacho* and feel reborn. Men are asleep in their cars in the shade of the car park.

I admire some good graffiti, leaving Zamora for the long road north. There are signs for Braganza in Portugal. I take a left, the N631, crossing the Río Esla which looks like a huge lake. This route seems to correspond perfectly with the curve outlined in Laurie's map. The small road is very straight and endless. It goes across dried-up, hot dust-blown plains, sometimes there are red-earth fields of green unripe corn, then red-earth fields of baby vines sprouting their lime green leaves on matt-black short stems. Towering above the lot are gigantic pylons of triangled steel, keeping electricity in motion. Over all the fields are wide-angled irrigation pipes shaped like huge upside down coat hangers on wheels. There would be no life here, without water. Occasionally I go past small pine forests.

I am thinking of Laurie walking along here, getting blisters on his feet. He met some German guys in Zamora, musicians who called themselves 'students', probably at the University of Life, they had already travelled around Spain once and were just about to do the same again. They showed Laurie where to get some sandals and gave his old boots away to a nearby beggar. Later that night, they played at the dance hall, which was a filthy and abandoned warehouse down by the river. Laurie was starving, but the only food here was beer or wine. Soon, he could hardly stand. This is when a girl asked him to dance. 'She just wrapped her damp arms around me, propped me snugly erect with her bosom, and away we went over the flapping floorboards as though skating on Venetian blinds'. Every time he felt like falling over some more, she became 'like scaffolding' supporting him, until he finally ended up back in his seat.

Once the Germans stopped playing, the party was quickly over. Heinrich, Rudi and Artur were from Hamburg. Artur was the bandleader and he had fixed up some food: roast kid and beans. However, he went off on a major coughing trip before the midnight feast. I reckon he had galloping TB. A bit sad really.

For me, the long straight road goes on and on. I stop by a forest to pee behind a tree, whilst Misty pees up one. We explore the place for a bit of wild-camping. There are deep ditches along the ground, presumably some underground irrigation system for the trees. That would be a bummer, falling asleep in one of these just when the farmers get their twice-weekly ration of water. One would wake up wet and very surprised!

There is an enormous notice saying, 'No camping, No loud noises. No open fires but 4x4 cars are acceptable'. Well, don't get me started. I have to break the rules and light the stove for a cup of tea. After that I set the keyboard up on the flapped-down backdoor. It fits perfectly. I am convinced Honda had me in mind when they designed this brilliant backdoor. I get the keyboard switched on and blast out Albert King songs at the top of my voice. There is no applause, only some small birds fluttering down a few branches to get a close-up of the keyboard. My hands are stiff from all the driving. I have played terribly badly and decide to pack up.

I have not seen another car since getting onto this road and resolve to remind myself of this next time I am stuck in a city traffic jam. Both the windows are open, and in the rear-view mirror Misty looks like Snoopy, ears flapping up in the hot wind. I wipe my face, wondering if I just heard the dog thinking. Is this madness setting in?

Suddenly a great white cloud rolls along the road and engulfs the car, visibility nil. We grind to a standstill. I have to wind up the windows. The cloud consists of white fluffy seeds, like an instant hailstorm of flying cotton wool showering dryly through the air. Then it has gone. Had I just imagined this? No, here are some of the seeds stuck to the seats. I leave them there, open the windows and take to the road once more. On and on. Here is a stork's nest on a telegraph pole. I realize that the car urgently needs some petrol. Oops, what an oversight. Should have dealt with that in Zamora. Now, it is a major worry. On and on goes the road.

Without warning, I am suddenly on a motorway, in the middle of high-up nowhere. I am jubilant. Motorway means petrol; they go hand in hand. This brand-new motorway is totally empty. It is all beginning to feel a little eery. I wonder if I might be sleep-driving and am actually dreaming this. The next moment, there are two biker Guardia waving me down. One steps forward.

'*Hola*', he says, '*papeles, no. Permiso de conducir.*'(Hi, car papers, no, driving licence). There is very little 'please' and 'thank you' in Spain. It is just not the done thing. For once, Misty is not growling and barking furiously from the back, planning to rip the officer's arms and legs off. As the guy looks at my English driving licence like a gorilla looking at a shard of mirror, I look at his gun. The black of the revolver's handle is all worn away to steely silver at the handle. Pointing at the fuel gauge, I ask if he reckons I have enough petrol to reach the next petrol station. He tells me, there is a small place nearby, Puebla de Sanabria, with a petrol station and, *Sí, hay un camping*,' (Yes, there's a campsite) 'km79'. I babble in broken Spanish, that I am so glad to have met him. My relief must be showing. He blushes behind his black shades.

Right enough, here is a sign for the village. I find the campsite straightaway. What brilliant coincidence! To top it all, it's only six euros a night, and I can pay with plastic when I leave. Hurray! There's a Spanish caravan, and a German lorry that looks like a glammed-up tank. Apart from that, there's no one. Bliss! Usually, I get the tent up before cooking, but not tonight. I park the stove on some perfect cement thing, ideal for cooking. I fry cubed, fat bacon, cut up a vast tomatoe, and '*schnipsel*' (German for 'finely cut') half a handful of garlic to sizzle with the lot. Topped with black pepper, the pan is almost overflowing. I cut civilised slices of Segovian bread on my wee breadboard from the Chinese '*todo*'(everything) shop, to soak up the deliciously fragrant juices. I had been dying for a hot dinner earlier in all that heat, for hundreds of miles. Over cups of tea, the sky turns from grey to dark-blue, looking like rain is on the way. I quickly set up the tent. It is lovely where I am here, near to the river. I can hear it behind the thick cypress hedge, gushing by. I have only just finished putting stuff into the tent when the rain starts. Now for the acid tent test. Will it hold out or start leaking everywhere?

I sit completely still. Indeed, I become a full-bellied Buddha being heavily still. I am so completely stilled-out, I almost swoon over sideways with stillness.

when she realises that she has forgotten her friends outside in the rain and they cannot open zips

I could swear I've just heard the dog thinking, split seconds before registering my own thought, that I have left 'the water of life', distilled by my friends, Mr Whyte and Mr Mackay, under the car next to the fresh milk.

The rain rolls down the tent walls, plop plop drop the drops.

I have read the safety label on the tent's one pocket about twelve times in a row. I won't bore you with all the details like '100% Nylon, no fireproof area or flame-retardant sprayed on cover and do not smoke, made in China'. It is without doubt that moment. That moment for a cigarette, when you can't move either way, need to consider your options, and finally chill out. The dog coughs and sneezes at the fag. I tell her it will keep the wee beasties away.

in that case i prefer that stinky lemon oil stuff

'Don't touch the walls, Mist!' I tell the dog.

one should never point out the obvious

Fed up with the attitude of the dog and dying for a dram, I crawl outside. I want to be the kind of person who does not leave their friends standing in the rain. I stand up. It has stopped raining. The air is filled with the gorgeous aroma of damp, warm earth. Misty is chasing something through the hedge. I rescue my friends. Back in the tent, after a small amount of faffing with clothes, I discover her, all curled-up wet dog, on my one luxury item, the little lacy white pillow, now grey and damp. Oh boy, who would have a dog!

The rest of the evening unveils itself into frogs quarking and silver poplar leaves swishing silently above, a church bell dinging faraway, a blackbird singing sonorous baritone. Now it is either just before 8 pm or probably nearly twenty to midnight.

18 May 2006

At 7 am I hear the German couple banging heavy metal onto heavy metal. Maybe they are doing some last minute welding of more useful gadgets to their big green lorry which looks fit to cross a desert or two. The two of them and both their big Alsatians have breakfast and leave. Now two Spanish people emerge from their caravan in slippers and dressing gowns, inspecting the thick hedge by the river only to discover a high fence. I eat the other half of bread with sardines and go off to explore the surroundings, passing a one-man tent, still closed up. I guess it must be the cyclist who arrived last night, shortly after me.

Misty and I go up to the village along a just discovered secret path out of the campsite, then down the road, across the long bridge and through some trees until we finally reach the river. There is a wide ridge of rocks across it where white water falls off, gushing and roaring, before rejoining the river. A small island the size of a large doormat is perched on the ridge. On it stands one tall tree. On the very top is a stork's nest with three long grey necks craning for food. Mum and Dad are gliding around, looking for some. Misty is in paradise, swimming like an otter to catch her floating stick. Will the river take it or can she speed-swim and catch it? Snap, she has got it and swims against the current, to clamber up the rocky riverside and throw the stick at my feet. This goes on for ages, again and again until my throwing arm begins to ache. I pick some thyme and wild rosemary growing all around. The fragrance makes me feel so hungry, I could bite bits out of the very ground I am standing on.

Back up in the village, I buy a loaf in a bakery shop, which is in a cellar. The young lady shopkeeper has just given a little girl a *'magdalena'* (square fairy cake) *'gratis'* (free), and the girl's grandmother is all smiles. They talk about stuff I do not understand, but we all smile a bit more before I take the steps back up to the street.

In the *'ferretería'* (ironmonger's) across the street, there is a very different atmosphere. A small woman is bent double over the stone steps down into the dark shop, placing books, papers and magazines onto the steps. She does not look up. Inside, I say, *'Buenos díaa'* into the general space. The woman straightens up. Her head stops where my shoulders begin.

'¿Que quieres?' (What do you want?) she asks gruffly. I feel this is a little blunt.

'Quisiera una bomba para mi estofa pequeña de camping. ¿Lo tiene?' (I would like a cartridge for my small camping cooker. Do you have one?) I ask, having rehearsed the question over and over again during the river walk.

'¿Una bomba?' the woman asks back, grimly shocked. Have I just asked her for a bomb?

'*Si, pero solo una bomba pequeña, para el camping.*'(Yes, but only a small bomb, for camping), I reply. Have I made the situation worse? She stares at me in disbelief, deeply in thought. Finally, something seems to have clicked.

'*¡Cartucho!*'(Cartridge!) the woman cries out and points into the general darkness at the back of the shop, telling me to look for it myself. Then she bends double again, arranging more magazines. I look around the pots and pans, rolls of string, bags of nails and screws, hammers, soup ladles, brooms, spades. I cannot see any camping gas. Then I discover the woman's husband doing his accounts with thin lips, behind a small counter.

'*Hola, tienes una cartucha pequeña...blah...blah...*' (Hi, have you got a cartridge etc), I blurt out.

'*¿Cartucha? No,*' replies the man. My heart is sinking. Thoughts of no tea or any cooked food crawl across my brain. The man frowns at me, a bitter expression on his face. '*Cartucha, no.*' he repeats, then bellows at me, '*¡CARRRR-TUUU-CHO!*' before disappearing into the dark of the shop. Should I just leave, I wonder. They don't seem to be having a good day here. Now the man returns, holding a small camping gas cartridge. Fantastic! Only 1.50 euros! In the Tarifa campsite they charged 4.50 euros for one, what a rip-off. I pass a blond guy crouching before a sunglasses stand, trying on shades. I feel like telling him, 'They do nothing for you, try a different pair,' but there has been enough negativity so far and I leave, just managing to get past the gruff *señora* and her steps covered in books and stuff. Phew, that was a tough one.

Back on site, there is no one, only the small single-person tent, zipped up. I get the fat bacon and tomato frying and seat myself in the plastic chair, eating directly from the frying pan. I still have no plate. Stuffing my face greedily, I am munching away, when the blond bloke from the *cartucho* shop materializes.

'Hi - I just thought - seeing we're the only people left here - I'd come and say hello,' he goes. I look up from my feast.

'Hello,' I mumble and continue eating. My mouth is full. He sits himself in the grass next to where Misty is tied. She growls at him. Rob introduces himself and tells us of his dogs back in Portugal. Misty is beginning to warm to him. I feel a bit guilty not offering the guy some food as I go on gobbling it all up. I make us a cup of tea. Wandering off a bit later, Rob suggests to meet up at the bar, once the siesta is over and the place is open, to have a beer.

I get on with the washing-up.

The wooden floor in the bar has a section made of glass bricks under which a small, lit-up waterfall roars. I take one look and step sideways. No way could I stand on it. Already I am getting dizzy. Over on the windowsill is an ancient rusty ring, the size of two horseshoes welded together, standing on three legs, a long handle sticking out from the circle. Aha, I imagine lighting a fire under that and getting the *paella* pot going, sticky pale yellow rice smelling of saffron, with bits of rabbit and other delicacies slowly broiling away. We take our beers outside to stare at the river gurgling over green moss and ferns covering huge, old rocks. We decide the bar must have been a watermill in days gone by. It is cold in the shade. I try a cigarette to warm me up. Rob used to smoke but packed it in. He tells me how he cycled through the oddest hail shower of fluffy white stuff. It got into his nose, eyes, ears, everywhere. I am really pleased that he had also experienced the same freaky cloud. Had it not been for his story and some seeds actually stuck to the car seat, I would have been obliged to question my sanity. We decide to have dinner together, at his place.

I bring a flat grey stone, perfect for a serving platter and chopping board, sardines, garlic, tomatoes, pepper, thyme and rosemary, and a small candle. He sits by his tent doing weird things with bits of string. I think it best not to ask. Then he produces a most excellent round loaf of rye bread and chops bits off with his pocket knife. We slice the tomatoes, squish the sardines, cut the garlic, and grind the pepper onto the hunks of bread, topped with the wild herbs. I am already munching away, when he takes his first bite.

'Haruomhmhmh,' Rob goes, and, 'Ohryeasfhfhmh,' and chewing more, 'Arnfmh, hmm,' his vocals doing musical acrobatics to accompany the tastes. I nearly drop my bread. Is it that good? I realize that I am in the presence of a musical eater, now making more orgasmic exclamations.

'God, that is so good, sardines with raw garlic, the pepper and herbs on the tomatoes, the bread, fantastic.' He takes another bite. 'Yesssh hrmmm mmm.' He is off again. Misty tilts her head from side to side, listening to Rob's foody expressions. Killer laughter starts to bubble up inside me until I can contain it no longer and it bursts out echoing around the empty campsite. Rob nearly chokes on his beer, then he eats more. I cannot believe my ears. We must sound like a couple of loonies falling off our perches in the falling light. We have more beers and light the candle. I have a few fags as he is telling me about his wee house in Portugal which he is restoring using traditional materials and building techniques.

'Have you been up at the castle?' he wants to know. I tell him that I haven't.

'Let's go tomorrow. You have to see the way they are restoring the pointing, it is criminal!' He is off on a passionate rant. Later we discuss his bike's trailer. Preparing for his cycling trip to England, he was desperate to get his hands on a trailer. The day before his departure, he met someone by chance who wanted to get rid of his bike trailer. Need I say more? A bit like Laurie when his fiddle broke and someone from out of nowhere gave him a new one! We have more beers, talking of ant life, radio-controlled caravans, and UFOs, as one does. Rob has rigged up some sound system with fancy small gadgets and what looks like a miniature windmill. Brilliant! The night has turned very cold, and we invite Mr Whyte and Mr Mackay to join us around the candle on the flat stone.

Back in the tent, I am wearing several jumpers and a vast rainbow-striped cardigan, a present from Janis. I am freezing. So freezing that I feel like calling across to Rob to bring his blanket over and join me, just for the warmth of it. But I'm in love with Laurie, so it's not on.

19 May 2006

Misty and I spend the morning rambling around by the river. The peace is exquisite. We buy another loaf of bread and return to the campsite. I have found a small dead snake on the secret path and I am planning to bring it back for my grandson when I notice that total mayhem has broken out. Piles of Dutch caravans are in the process of arriving and setting up. One caravan almost falls onto its backend as it is disengaged from the tow bar, another is neatly radio-controlled into place. Tables are unfolded, chairs brought out and set down, awnings put up, followed by the click-clacking of poles and the squeaking of stretched plastic. My instinct tells me to move immediately. I pick the milk up from under the car and put it and the cooking stuff into the back. I pick up the zipped up tent by the cross of its two poles at the top and carry it away, to a small bay, far away, with a view of the river as well as the stork's nest. Today there are only two chicks. Has that falcon cruising the nest this morning stolen one? I have lost a tent peg and use a knife instead. Leiff always checks the ground when campers have left, and he has a whole collection of spare pegs. I could do with one now. I go back and get the car. A regular village of white eggs-on-wheels has built up around it. I am dead chuffed that I have moved and return to my new place. I set about making a kind of salad creation with pieces of tomato, white beans from a jar, and a small tin of tuna tipped over the lot with herbs from the riverside for my Friday feeling. Over cups of tea, I get the chance of some more people-watching. A group of Dutch caravanners have just appeared and disappeared in the undergrowth of the hedge, the men dividing the thick cypress branches to get a look at the river, with the women standing by doing nothing. Ah, the tall fence is discovered. We've all been there. I had been there too, soon after my arrival, trying to gain access to the river from this side. It is impossible. Now I have the only place 'with a view', the only break in the needly hedge.

'I've seen it!' Rob is grinning from ear to ear. 'My first radio-controlled caravan! It's true! I couldn't believe my eyes!' We go up through the village, over cobblestones, up steep narrow streets and small lanes, past old houses with bright geraniums, a tourist shop with a life-size stuffed bear outside and some T-shirts with pictures of wolves on the front. Here two happy young men ask me what type of dog Misty Blue is.

'Ah, Borrrder Collie.' They roll their tongues in unison. '*¡Pensamos que la perra era un Husky o un lobo pequeño de cerca de aquí!* (We thought the bitch was a Husky or a small wolf from around here!) I am surprised that Misty has not snapped at them or bitten their hands off. Instead she is loving being stroked by them and bathing in their adoration.

Rob and I wonder how the place feels so affluent,

where does the money come from to have houses so well kept, new window frames and all. We reckon there must be a lot of tourism in the summer. Rumour has it that there is even another campsite, by the big lake a few kilometres away. It is bound to be more expensive than our site. Here we are at the castle now.

'Look at this,' thunders Rob. 'It's an outrage; look!' He is running his fingers along the cemented sins. 'This is concrete. Concrete, I ask you. This should be lime!' The pointing between the granite blocks does look a bit out of style. He shows me more patches of the peculiar repair work, his anger steadily rising. 'How can this be allowed?'

The little castle is open and there is no charge to look around. Upstairs, Rob and I imagine hordes of enemies on horseback approaching from the valley below as we are peering through the arrow-slits in the walls.

'Shut the castle gates! Bring more arrows!' Rob shouts to no one downstairs.

I call out, 'Boil the oil! Fetch water from the well!' We fire imaginary arrows at the invisible oncoming riders in battle gear. On the other side of the castle we imagine peasants who have taken to the mountains in the distance.

'You couldn't fit all the people from an entire village in here, could you?' wonders Rob aloud. 'Or could you?'

I don't think so. The place is really small and you probably had to be some kind of noble person, worthy of preservation, rather than just any old peasant with his donkey. But who am I? I don't actually have a clue. We discover a beautiful little house on the hillside, for sale, and are considering moving in when I notice that it is not pointing west, but east instead, so no sunsets on the porch. That does it. We move on admiring massive, old, grey roof slates, the size of large fridge doors. The landscape roundabout is all rugged mountains intercut by vast shrubby plains. Wolves are supposed to be roaming these wild distant hills and forests.

In the evening I am just settling down to pick hundreds of white dog hairs from the black cardigan when Rob shows up with dinner, a whole lot of beers. Naturally, I immediately change my plan, and we talk through the night, about bike-trailer design, how to make a solar cell out of an old laptop and other useful stuff, the river rushing by. The castle is lit up in fabulous orange hues, its silent mysteries still hidden within.

20 May 2006

I wake up to a clear blue sky and decide this is a washing day. Next to the bathrooms is the washing room with rows of deep sinks, ridges at one end, to scrub the clothes. Ah, no sink plugs. Spanish people seem to have a secret passion for sink plugs; they take them away, don't ask me why. I discover to my delight that the lid of a five litre water bottle fits perfectly into the drain and set about scrubbing away at the pine needle sap stain et cetera, all the while doing my voice warming-up exercises. They go a bit like this, 'aaaaheeeeeeehiiiiiiiiiiuuuuuuuaaah' or breathing in and 'ooooohiiiiiiieeeeehaaaaoooh' with appropriate facial contortions, when this head appears at the edge of the open door. By this time I am doing the 'onetwohthrreefohfihve without breathing in more fivfohthrrreetwoonne' up and down bit. The head has gone.

Back at my place, I put up the washing line made of red parcel string between the hedge and a handy little tree. Once the wet clothes are on the line, it breaks. I hang the heavy things over the open car doors and put more of them on the roof and bonnet. I fix the line with a deft knot and hang up lighter things like socks and stuff. I have only brought two washing clips, otherwise known as clothes pegs, which is a bit of an oversight really. Then I'm off to raid the shop on the other side of the river for some cigarettes. On my return the heat has become terrific and I decide to do a bit of sunbathing in my strawberry bikini after luncheon which was exactly the same as the day before. Soon, I have to get out the orange and pink sun umbrella. I hammer it into the hard ground with the small breadboard. The breadboard falls apart, into four short neat lengths of wood. I should have used the hammer! I settle myself down on my turquoise tablecloth/scarf/skirt and watch a shiny jet-black carpenter beetle with its brilliant blue hues glittering in the sun, idly crawling along. This is the life! Feeling 'fat with time', I am just about to doze off when Rob appears with biscuits covered in white chocolate. I put on the tablecloth for a skirt and fire up the kettle for afternoon cups of tea. We get the maps out, discussing routes and places to go. Rob had only meant to stay one night, so now he is in a bit of a hurry to get to Santander by Thursday.

I had been told by my Swedish friend back in Edinburgh about the Picos de Europa, the high mountains in the north, apparently the first sign of Europe when you are coming by boat from America. '*Pico*' can mean anything from 'mouth', 'mountain peak', 'spout', to 'penis', and sailors would make rude remarks the moment the 'Picos' became visible. We discuss the journeys of Columbus and why he did not turn left or right when he reached the sea, but instead went straight ahead, - was he looking for Asia? We agree that he knew exactly what he was doing, and he had the courage to prove his theory of a round world. We imagine life on board the small sailing ships of the time. The dangerous expeditions must have been horrendous with a cramped lifestyle worse than camping; at sea for eight months! Unbearable!

I show Rob the four sticks that used to be the breadboard.

'Perfect for starting a small fire. We should steal some of those logs by the secret path and light a fire when it gets colder,' he says, but we don't actually dare.

On the way to the toilets, we come across the Dutch people having a party. The smells from their barbecues are overwhelming, and there is even a Spanish man playing a guitar, singing mournful flamenco songs.

'I would like a party with everyone dressed up as Saxons, eating roast ox and pig from a spit by a huge fire, everyone throwing the bones over their shoulders and drinking ale from drinking horns, falling asleep on the table and waking up to start drinking more beer. I love food and beer...' Rob is getting carried away a bit by the lovely food smells.

I smell the big blue iris flowering nearby. Its smell reminds me of violets. We have some more biscuits and beer. The mosquitoes are getting lively and I grab the lemon oil. This evening, there is no silvery shine on the poplar leaves by the river. I feel rain in the air.

'Ah, good. Rain would be good for cycling; it would be cooler,' says Rob cheerfully.

We talk and talk. Finally I pluck up the nerve to ask him about the bits of string.

'Ah, that. Well, I decided to take a book on my journey, as a luxury thing sort of. My sister gave it to me. It's all about knots, how to tie different types of knot. Not really that exciting but good for the concentration. I have been practising knotting with the strings and I know six different ones already.' He laughs. Suddenly fireworks go off on the other side of the river. Bang, hiss. Misty has fled into the tent and is shooting about like a wild viper looking for cover. I stuff the sleeping bag over her ears and put her on the lead. We do not want another 'wolf experience'. The multi-coloured fireworks reflect in the river, its little waves making the colours look all wobbly. Rob and I have a cheers inspection straightaway to celebrate our last evening together in style. The whisky goes down a treat. We resolve that if I wake up before him in the morning I am to shout loud abuse at his tent at once.

21 May 2006

Rob is ready to leave by the time I have had my second cup of tea. All the Dutch have already gone. I kiss Rob's cheek 'cheerio' and 'safe journey', and he blushes like a blond man.

After another cold night I am today in my big walking boots, fat socks and several layers of T-shirts and jumpers. Trinny and Susannah would positively cringe at the style or lack of it, but needs must. The sky is grey. I charge up my mobile in the hairdryer plugs at the toilets while I have about twelve showers, one after the other, with lots and lots of hot water. I seem to be shedding layers of dried-up skin. A lovely warm shower with white tiles, pink curtains, and a new, clean, warmed-up me. I forget to pick up the shampoo and conditioner and when I return later, they have gone.

Following a huge Sunday breakfast of six slices of fat bacon, two fried eggs, four pieces of yesterday's bread, toasted in the gas-stove flame and four big cups of tea, I take the dog for a long walk. The weather is brightening up. First, I check on the storks. There are still only two chicks visible, and the big falcon with white armpits is back, looking hungry. I am coming over all maternal, my mind screaming rude things at the raptor, to chase it off in no uncertain terms. It ignores me.

i could scare it or distract it go on throw this stick into the river

Oh dear, this time I really heard the dog thinking. I pick up the stick and whack it through the air into the river. I am a pretty rubbish thrower but this is a good one. The falcon buzzes off as Misty shoots into the river, barking madly. Where are Mum and Dad stork? Probably looking for frogs. Then I see it. A silver parcel lying in the grass. It is a massive piece of untouched chorizo, manna from heaven! It goes directly into my satchel. Someone must have forgotten it here last night, when there was the fireworks party.

Further down the river, a man has just caught a good-sized fish.

'*Madre mía, Santa María, no lo creo, gracias, madre mía, gracias*' (Mother of mine, Holy Mary, I don't believe it, thank you), the fisherman exclaims loudly, admiring his catch, neatly netted. Misty sees the fish too, flapping silvery in the air before landing in the net.

me too i want to catch a fish like that

She rushes off into the river and starts diving under. The entire dog has disappeared in the water. Like a pearl diver she must be holding her breath, looking for fish under the surface of the water. We walk for miles and back again. I have four tangerines sitting on a rock by the river. The monotony of my diet is becoming a bit boring, but I think myself lucky at my abundance of food in comparison to Laurie. He had 'fried eggs and purple wine' somewhere near here or 'a mouthful of mineral water and several glasses of sherry' to help him recover from sunstroke. In Zamora, he had disgusting-sounding 'pink effervescent juice', reminding him of hair oil and, just before the night of the wolf attack, he had a dinner of bread and dates. Rob had dates, but I prefer tomatoes. Spanish tomatoes are simply fantastic. I wake up from my daydreaming and notice that I have lost the dog's lead. This means that we have to do the whole distance again to find it. Eventually I find it, lying in the grass. That was lucky! But now for the long trek back. The sun is heating up and I unpeel some jumpers. My feet are boiling. Trudge, trudge. I pick some more thyme and rosemary and even discover some watermint. That will make a nice change for the tomato dinner later. Now, whole families have come fishing. Young couples take happy Sunday afternoon pictures of each other. I trudge back over the long bridge, don't look down, vertigo, uphill to the village, down the secret path, back to the tent. I urgently need tea, and I am almost faint with hunger. While the kettle is boiling with water for tea and two eggs for dinner, I sink my teeth into a large tomato and eat it like an apple. The other one gets the mint treatment. There is no one around at all.

In the bathrooms a little later, I plug the keyboard into the hairdryer plug and play a bit of Bach, still getting stuck at the same bit near the end after all these years, then it's on to 'Summertime' and 'House of the Rising Sun'. I need to practise more but give up for the moment. Good sound in the room full of listening toilets, showers and sinks.

At the ranch, I get out Laurie's book and dream a bit. I wonder how far Rob has got by now. I have a wee dram to help me wonder.

Inside the tent, the smell of my feet shatters my space. Too lazy to walk to the bathroom, I fling my socks outside and cover up my feet. I wonder why the stench has not poisoned the dog, now either dead, or asleep.

During the night, I hear a distant train rattling by. I hope it is not carrying nuclear waste.

22 May 2006

I wake up with freezing wet feet, the tent flapping in the rain, the thick shawl protecting my notes soaking wet. The weather seems to have gone all circular, one moment it's all hot sun, the next there's rain and a bitter wind blowing. I rearrange the stuff in the car in case the rain persists and I decide to sleep in the back of the car. You never know.

On this Monday morning, I'm off to explore the other side of the village. Walking uphill I want to find a village called 'Lobozeros' (Wolf catchers?) in the Sierra de la Cabrera (Sierra of the goatherdess). The first thing I discover is a railway station, closed. At least the mystery of the nightly train sounds are unfolded. Moving on swiftly, along a single track road with some passing places, the landscape reminds me of the Scottish Highlands: vast spaces of hills and mountains covered in shrubby vegetation. A strong wind has got up and cleared the sky. The sun is getting into its own once more, and soon I have to sit down by the road to get rid of my jumper. Hot or what! Here on a rock is some heather growing. Heather? I kid you not. I had no idea that heather grows in Spain. Feeling a bit of an idiot, I walk on. One car passes by, the post van. I should have hitched a lift. There are no houses in the distance, nothing. It is too hot to walk the next eight miles. I give up on my plan to find the village I wanted to see, only because its name contains the word 'wolf', and it has a restaurant named '*casa de lobos*' (house of wolves). I sit myself down in a rubbish dump. I love a good rummage in a rubbish dump. Surveying broken toilets, a single old shoe, a heap of broken tiles and flowerpots over a cup of tea from the thermos, I suddenly discover a whole lot of cast-out slate roof tiles. Some still have rusty ancient nails stuck in them, and here are the old roof beams, with woodworm and almost sun-bleached white. I resolve to return with the car and steal some of these enormous slates to bring to my kids as a souvenir from wolf country. Yes, dear reader, you might think what a shame, those poor kids, being landed with great big slabs of slate. But they have been landed with a pretty peculiar mother all these years, so not to worry.

Back through the village, I buy a loaf of bread and a pastry delight which I balance delicately back to the tent. It has gone.

I park the cake on top of the car and go looking for the tent. It has blown into the bushes in a faraway corner of the hedge. Phew. At least it is still there! I carry it back to its pitch and even find a spare tent peg. After the cake fest, I have a lazy cigarette, sitting outside the tent in the sun. The dog is in the shadow of the hedge, the shiny silver cake tray which she had licked clean earlier near her nose. She has just dozed off when this massive magpie lands directly next to her, its big black beak pecking at the tray. I cannot believe my eyes. Has this bird no sense of fear? As if the dog can hear me thinking, Misty opens her eyes. Shocked, the magpie takes off, but only to a few yards away. It is in love with the silver cake tray glittering in the hot sunlight. What attracts magpies to shiny things to the point of having to take them to their nests, I wonder. No other birds go crazy stealing silver paper, even whole teaspoons.

Here is lawnmower man now wearing a biker's jacket in gaudy red, blue and white worn leather patterns. He is not so much cutting the grass as watching the big yellow machine do it for him, following it idly. They are approaching fast. I am beginning to feel invaded by petrol fumes and the noise of the machine. The smells of spring in the air are destroyed as butterflies flee, flowers bend their heads and birds are flushed out of the hedge shouting their disapproval. A woman's voice - his wife? - is shouting disapproval from the distance.

'*¡Pero - quítate de ahí*!' (But - get away from there!), and he does!

As the hot afternoon is turning to dusk, countless birds sing a late dawn chorus.

23 May 2006

I vaguely remember the church bells going at 4 am, there was no dawn chorus, only total silence, even the river seemed to be asleep. It was pretty cold, probably too cold for the birds to sing, and the dog kept trying to get into the sleeping bag.

It is my hand that gets the surprise first, feeling frozen cloth with clumps of stuck-on hail or ice (?) as I open the zip of the mosquito-net doors. The outer two cloth doors, neatly tied to the tent poles, are covered in ice. The entire tent and the car are covered in frost! I cannot believe my eyes. There is a layer of ice on Misty's drinking water. My fingers are frozen stiff, and I can hardly turn on the wee stove for a cup of tea. At the toilets, there is ice melting on the bathroom roof and water dripping down with great plops. I have a sudden craving for meat. Meat, I want to eat meat! The thin sickle-shaped moon is fading from the totally clear bright blue sky. There is no wind, and the river is steaming, sliding along like fresh, black crude oil. This day is going to be a boiler! I am wearing almost all my clothes, except for the bikini, and look like the Incredible Hulk. After some tea and toasted old bread with olive oil, I drive through the village, to astonished looks of other early risers staring at my ice-scraped windows. Unperturbed, I go off to steal some of the huge roof slates.

Back on site, the morning sun has made silver leaves on the poplar trees. Everything seems steeped in the shiny magic of a fairy tale. I venture off to the village, making heavy footprints on the frozen path, grimly intent on hunting for meat. A tiny tanned man emerges from his van. His ears stick out from his head almost at right angles but he makes the best of it and gaily balances a small turquoise cap on them. Passing him, he gives me the 'I'll leave the key under the mat for you anytime' look and nearly swallows the stump of cigar sticking to his sun-dried lips. Whatever brought that on?

The *señora* tells me the meat has not yet come, I should come back later.

'You make camping?' she asks in Spanish. I tell her about the frost and ice, and she is all *'madre mia'* astonishment, incorporating dramatic, theatrical body language of being frozen to death whilst asleep. I wander around the village wondering how to raise some cash for some lovely rustic-looking pots I have admired for days in a shop window. Perhaps I'll remember the four numbers for some expensive credit card cash by tomorrow.

The swifts are flying overhead, and it is now warm enough to de-hulk. As I get rid of some more clothes, I notice a small German camper van arriving at the site. The heat is rising with incredible speed. By lunchtime, the air is almost at boiling point. I have always wanted to try this, so I put the frying pan on the roof of the car, to fry an egg on it. It works! However, it is fried at the bottom as well as the top, a rock solid fried-on-car egg. I am not that keen on solid fried eggs, so I give it to Misty and decide on my next experiment.

Using the empty tin of '*pulpo*'(squid in its black ink) which I had had for luncheon, and quite a disgusting one at that except for the tomato, I mix together an egg yolk and some drops of olive oil, producing organic hair conditioner. In the showers, I wash my hair with washing-up liquid '*lavavajillas*', and proceed to pour my invention over my head. I instantly smell like an omelette. Is the hot shower cooking the stuff onto my head? No, it just smells like it. Now the eggnog without the nog is running rawly into my eyes, my ears, down my back. Absolutely double gross! Dear reader, do not try this at home, it positively sucks!

I dry my hair in the hot sun, relieved that there are no bits of solid egg yolk glued to it. What I don't know is that my dried-out sun-bleached hair is sticking out from my head like the stiff red wig of a clown, horizontally. Combined with the fading red wine stain of the ex-tortoise on my face, I must look quite a sight. I am unaware of this. Walking past the German camper van, I notice a small mature lady sitting in the sun, reading a guide to Spain.

'*Guten Tag, wie geht's*!'(Hi, how are you), I call across to her. She looks up and instantly leaps into her van, hiding behind the door curtain. I can only see her small feet. Misty wants to chase her. Bit by bit, the woman's head appears as she is tightly holding on to the curtain.

'*Ja, umgotteswillen, Sie haben mir aber einen Schreck eingejagt*!'(For God's sake, you really gave me a fright!), she says, her voice a bit wobbly. '*Was ist denn mit Ihrem Haar los*?(What is the matter with your hair?)

Are you English? You look as if you've stuck your head into the National Grid!' She emerges from the van cautiously. I tell her about my egg-s-perience. She assures me it did not work and lends me her conditioner. Off back to the showers, I put sweet smelling chemicals on my head.

Rika, the van-lady, and I spend the afternoon exploring the village around the castle. It is closed. She invites me to the coffee-shop-bakery for a treat of wonderful cake and *café con leche*. We have a lot in common, both having married 'abroad' and even having lived in Edinburgh's Marchmont area at similar times! What gets me about coincidence is that there is no such thing. Stuff doesn't just randomly happen; it is all planned. Maybe by angels. What do we know?

Over a delicious bottle of wine in her camper van with all mod cons, even a vase of fresh wild flowers clipped to the dashboard; she tells how she has been 'on the road' for four years. In all that time she has never met another woman travelling alone. She is not entirely a spring chicken at seventy-one years old. It turns out that she set up an organisation in Munich - Frauen Wohnen e.G. - for women only, to buy into a totally female-living community. Men are permitted to stay but cannot buy apartments in the big complex. Waiting for it to be built, having done four years of planning, organising and finally, successfully, presenting the proposals to the city council of Munich for some financial support, Rika took to the road. This autumn, she will move into her new home, a three-minute walk from a beautiful grand lake; yet after four years on the road, she is loathe to leave the gypsy lifestyle.

Usually, I have a bit of an attitude problem with Mercs

and their drivers, though not this time. Rika rocks, and 'Hati', the white lady elephant, her spacey miniature white Merc mobil, is a darling.

We look at lots of maps. She has loads of fantastic small-scale maps with all sorts of detail, guide books, poetry books even, little elephant figurines walking about here and there, and she is astonished at my complete lack of travel planning. All I have is Laurie's hand-drawn map and my 'old one', of the whole of Europe. Laurie did no planning, so neither do I. Taken aback, Rika shakes her head and thinks I'm crazy. Well, one man's poetry is another man's poison. Normally, I prefer to plan things out too, but as I am driving in the footsteps of a romantic dead poet, I had to forget planning, trying to enact a similar style of travel to Laurie Lee's and accepting wherever the wind blew me. Not knowing where I would end up, having merely marked the purple line on my old map to match Laurie's route, I wanted to empathise with him. Feel his feelings and live a bit like he might have lived, with very little money and hungry. On the whole, I think many German people like to plan ahead, nailing everything down in advance to avoid feelings of insecurity. The notion of just 'walking out, some midsummer morning' is therefore completely alien. Being a 'born and bred' German myself, it was an extra challenge for me not to plan ahead. A challenge of testing my nerve, which I thought would somehow make me stronger. Rika is perplexed at this. We wish each other good luck, and I depart.

Later, I am in the bar with the glass floor to pay my bill with plastic as I am leaving early the next morning. I ask the lawnmower man about wolves. 'Why all the T-shirts with wolf pictures on them? Are there any real ones around?' (I am sorry for my rocky use of the Spanish language.)

'Oh yes,' he replies, 'there are wolves, but only in the Sierras. Not as many as in the old days, but wolves, yes, definitely. But you have brought your own!' he jokes as I am leaving.

The lonely blackbird sings into the evening. The river rushes by. I feel a degree of melancholia rising, the journey with my dead poet possibly ending tomorrow. I don't want it to, and feel I am only just beginning, having walked out early one May morning. It is quite hard to be in love with a dead poet.

But I've still got it bad and I know it's here to stay. I have not heard the dog think anything all day, but tonight I know she wants to run with the wolves. Dogs or wild wolves are howling somewhere, far away, in the darkening night. It is time for a cheers inspection. Mr Whyte and Mr Mackay assure me that every morning I shall walk out, early or not, like good friends who always restore confidence. I drink the whisky in the manner of 'the housekeeper', whilst Don Quixote dies in a fever lasting six days before emerging as his new, or 'real' self, Alonso Quixano.

24 May 2006

Just getting out of the village after tea, bread and sardines, I learn that here, in beautiful fantastic Puebla de Sanabria, some vandals opened the reservoir, fed by the glacial lake, sometime in the 1950s, and over three hundred people drowned within minutes.

Reader. I got the cash. The man selling me the gorgeous handmade casserole pots tells me more about the place, or possibly himself. 'It is dead here. At least in the summer there are some more people, but it is dead here. A dead village place. There is no life. I want to be in Madrid, please God, somewhere with some life!' We are matching lids to the red-clay, half-glazed pots. 'Yes, they are made just down the road, in the village called Pereruela, from the red earth around here. You can put them over an open flame or in the oven.' He changes gear and starts making sheep and cow noises to describe what to roast in the pots. 'Yes, this was a shop for selling cloth, before; it is very old.' The curved wooden counter has an opening flap under which the floorboards seem paper thin.

The pots look like they have been made before the

invention of the potter's wheel. The clay has many rough bits to it, and the handles of the dishes look like a four-year-old has squished them into shape. He packs them into boxes from his sister's shop, next door. I have given up hurrying, and wait. There is a great big hole in the old shop's worn floorboards, bouncing lightly underfoot, near the front door. The place feels more alive with '*antigüedad*' (antiquity) than the castle. I pay and go, about fifty yards down the steep cobblestone road to the village fountain. Here, I fill up my five litre plastic water things from the fountain tap, and get on the road.

Swerving up and over, to catch up with the asphalt, I stop immediately at the petrol station. A man is cleaning his lorry's windscreen with a stiff broom and jets of water. I get the car tanked up with plastic money and go.

The brand-new road curves through the mountains. There is a harsh Alpine whiff on the air. We have left the fields of green wheat; the colours of the mountaintops here are a burnt-out grey. I am mulling over Oscar's story, the pot seller, who had also heard the dogs, or wolves, howling in the distance last night. His '*abuelo*'(grandad) went about with a coach and horses, and always took his rifle as packs of wolves would rush up to the moving coach, trying to attack the horses! The only thing that scared them off was fire. The area between Zamora and Puebla de Sanabria had the most wolves in the whole of Spain. Now there are still quite a few left, but they are a protected species.

About a hundred kilometres up the road I see signs for Xinzo de Limía. I reckon it is somewhere around here that Laurie spent his first night in Spain, sleeping in a crater among the rocks, rolled inside a blanket, his rucksack for a pillow. But sleep was not to be.

'I was attacked by wild dogs - or they may have been Galician wolves. They came slinking and snarling along the ridge of my crater, hackles bristling against the moon, and only by shouting, throwing stones, and flashing my torch in their eyes was I able to keep them at bay. Not till early dawn did they finally leave me and run yelping away down the hillside, when I fell at last into a nightmare doze, feeling their hot yellow teeth in my bones'.

I am puzzled as to how Laurie walked more than a hundred kilometres on his first day in Spain. Impossible; he must have got a lift or two from someone along the way. Mist and I have gone through the thirteenth tunnel and are suddenly in Galicia. Purple patches of flowering heather and full-bloom yellow gorse cover the mountains. Many are forested, some shaved clean of trees. The heavy coconut perfume of blossoming gorse pervades the air. It is absolutely heavenly. I set about making tea in a field, boiling two eggs in the same water, the sun beating down and almost melting the mayonnaise on the crunchy bread.

Vigo hits on us like electric shock therapy during meditation. It is a forest of skyscrapers with a few Alpine-looking houses, mad traffic fighting along the streets. I stop in the Parque do Castro so Misty can run about a bit, but I don't bother with the castle. After two days on a ship, Laurie arrived in Vigo in the early morning. 'It seemed to rise from the sea like some rust-corroded wreck, as old and bleached as the rocks around it,' he says. There were people sleeping in doorways as Laurie noticed 'mysterious graffiti' on some crumbling walls and a photo of 'Marx in a barbershop'.

'I suddenly felt the urge to get moving,' Laurie goes on,

and I couldn't have put it better myself. Apparently, Vigo has Europe's biggest fishing fleet. Well, the harbour stinks of dead fish, all the cranes are grey, and I have to pay (sixty-five cents) to get out of here. Just after 2 pm, the tourist information office is closed and, I assume, Laurie has been forgotten.

There are some small islands, the 'Islas Cies', rising from the sea near Vigo. I believe, only tenting campers are permitted to stay overnight. I like that. Also, a beautiful suspension bridge catches my eye on the way out of town as well as an old stone house that must have stood here, even during Laurie's time.

Now for a bit of background. Oh dear. In November 2002, about 250 kilometres west of Vigo, disaster struck when a huge oil tanker, the 'Prestige', started leaking oil and then sank. Two 'black tides' left the 'Costa da Morte', from A Coruña to Fistera, covered in thick black sludge. The National Park of the 'Islas Atlánticas' was destroyed. It took three weeks to suck up the 14,000 tons of oil from the sea. Thousands of volunteers helped the workers to clean up. The damage to the environment, fish and seafood stock was incredible. The Spanish government took over two weeks to think about it before bringing in the army to organize cleaning up the mess.

I turn left somewhere after Pontevedra in the vague hope of finding a campsite. Beautiful forests and lovely small villages with many new houses, but no camping anywhere. I feel a bit scared to forest wild-camp in this ordered little world and move on to Santiago de Compostela.

It is rush hour here, yet, after a short while, I find the one campsite, near the airport, north-east of the city. Hurray! The bulky, non-speaking *señora* charges me twelve euros for the night, and I set up the tent. Off for an evening walk, I have a cigarette under a massive eucalyptus tree, a sign stuck to its massive trunk, '*se vende*' (for sale). Is this a joke? A tree for sale? I have dinner here, a tuna-mayo sandwich and you've guessed it, a large tomato, enjoying the peace and watching a nosy robin watching me.

Back on site, I realize that I have camped next to the M6 of the campsite. Everyone and their dogs walk past, and back again. I can't be bothered to find a quieter spot. It is 10 pm and dark. Here are two Dutch guys now, stopping to stare, like two little boys admiring a Lotus, at a vast, newly arrived French camper van, the size of a bus. Stare, discuss, point. Suddenly there are fireworks going off in the town. This in turn sets off all the dogs on the site, barking. Misty flies around the tent. Techno music mixes with distant traffic noises. Drunk Germans tell me some people have cycled here from Ireland, but I cannot find them. In the lit-up 'bus/castle', a very, very large lady munches something over a board game. How does she fit into the built-in toilet without getting stuck? I wish my mind would mind its own business. From the town, the sounds of U2 are wafting across. I don't believe it: there is a big rock concert going on. Fantastic! Mr Whyte and Mr Mackay join me to party on.

and i got a tick on my eyelid at luncheon dog she was quick picking that one off it is all very green here with familiar looking weeds she still looks like a witch on wheels with that white hair sticking from her head and what about the size of that moth at the toilet door this morning i nearly freaked when she tied the lead right close to it the size of a small bird it was with creamy white beige brown markings on long spread out fancily pointed wings trouble was it had the eyes of an owl and i was glad when she got back

It's amazing; nobody thinks I'm here because I am in total darkness. My phone rings but I don't answer it; I do not want to be a dark tent, talking loudly to invisibility.

25 May 2006

I dreamt of Rika, the 249 elephants collection woman, and her remarks about the cream cakes in Sanabria. *'Windbeutel*? (Windbags?) *Nein, das sind ja Sturmsaecke*! (No, those are Storm Sacks!)

I had meant to be the first person up with the birds and away, but the blond German with his VW van has beaten me to it. By 8.30 I am at the cathedral. It is a cold, overcast morning, Santiago is still sleeping. A woman beggar stands holding out her empty hand by the cathedral gates. I check the two large stone scallop shells, symbol of the pilgrims, high above the door.

Inside, the place is awe-inspiring. All the gold and silver of the altar get on my nerves immediately. A nun is faffing about, gently slapping around fat candlesticks with a feather duster. There are eight confession boxes in a row looking as if eight Dr Whos are presently going to step out of them. Eight guys in holy men's attire wander in. There are two enormous organs on opposite walls. Wow, stereo organs, that must be a right ear fest. People kneel and cross themselves before sitting down. Some, dressed in mountaineering gear with posh new walking sticks and scallop shells tied around their necks, are just standing around. Japanese-looking people take pictures of everything, digitally extending their camera arms.

The eight priests start some chanting and eventually one of them reads from the bible, kisses it, '*los palabras del Dios*' (the words of God), and the congregation keeps getting up and sitting down again. A Spanish woman behind me yawns. One organ strikes up and blows me away. What a sound! Imagine two of them together! Double wow! An invisible man sings as if he has forgotten to warm up his voice, nasally, thinly. The woman behind me yawns again, loudly.

After some more getting up and sitting down and the priest going on from up on a small pulpit, she yawns again. It must have been a good night. Maybe she went to the concert.

It's time for the body and blood of Jesus, and the priest eats the biscuit and takes a good slug of the wine. It is not yet 10 am. Suddenly people rush forward, their hands held in prayer, to take the body of Christ and all that.

Meanwhile, high up behind the altar, a constant train of people move across the back of it, human hands hugging the golden Saint Iago statue by the throat, while the service continues. After the food and drink, everybody shakes hands. A monk in a wine-red cloak collects money into a small cloth sack. I check out the dangling rope mechanism for the incense burner or '*botafumeiro*'.

In a flash of rushing cassocks, eight wine-red-dressed monks are gathered in a small circle each holding one of the eight ropes coming from a massive rope, attached to the *botafumeiro*. This is the biggest incense burner in the world. Something smells strongly of soap bar. Then I notice it, the *botafumeiro*, the size of my car engine, gently gliding either side of the altar. As the monks pull harder on their rhythmic ropes, the pot takes on gigantic momentum until it positively speeds through the air, going higher and higher, faster, faster, whooshshsh, whooshshsh, from one side of the cathedral the size of a football pitch to the other, high up, smoking powerfully through the air. People gush Aahh's and Oohh's all over the place, staring up at the massive smoke-pot flying from side to side, their heads all turning in unison, following its directions.

Suddenly, it's all over. The priests go off; only a monk is left with a shovel full of the still burning, red-hot embers of incense.

Behind the altar, I too touch the golden scallop shell of Saint Iago's statue and then see a monk sitting behind me, constantly making hugging motions to the passing people. All this pomp and circumstance of Catholicism brings on a Victor Meldrew grumble, yet something has profoundly touched me.

I immediately drive off, for what seems like hundreds of miles, in the wrong direction. I put this down to the smoke. From what I have seen and heard and smelled of Santiago, I think I could live here. The beautiful buildings in the old town with its polished, old, cobblestoned streets and alleys, the tiny windows of colourful bars, all gave me feelings of peculiar harmony to the point that I could have kissed the pavement. I could even have forgiven the stall holders outside the cathedral, selling rosaries and walking sticks with scallop shells tied to them. Glad that I bought a baguette and slices of manchego cheese on my way out of town, I am presently tearing bits from both whilst driving out of town. Can one get fined for this? It is illegal to talk on a mobile phone when driving a car. But at least I am not holding the bread to my ear or talking to the cheese.

Back on track, I remind myself that I should never start a day without some breakfast. The rush this morning had been a mistake. Yet I might have missed the rare, spectacular ceremony at the Cathedral had I lingered on. I am presently going towards La Coruña (the crown). Once nearly there, I ask myself why. Rika had read her guide to me about the place and the area. It has Europe's most fantastic and stunning beaches et cetera. It sounded expensive somehow. So I turn towards Ferrol, where Franco, 'The Butcher of Asturias', was born. Then I decide in the last minute of motorway exits to take the coast road, along the 'Costa Verde' (Green Coast). I have been through nineteen tunnels, but one of them twice by now, because I must have gone in a circle. I put this down to the smoking incense more, when all of a sudden, I take in the most fabulous view of sea and cliffs and rocks. The grey clouds tear open; here is the sun and blue sky with puffy fog rising into it from the fjord-like cliffs.

With rush hour in Viveiro and everyone going back to work at 5 pm, I am lost again. Once I have found the campsite at Viveiro, it is closed. The perfectly made-up woman in some sweety kiosk tells me to come back in June, or go to Foz. I recognize the symptoms of severe tea-shortage and brew up in the car park.

Aha, Fernando was absolutely right. Foz is the place to go. A place name, dear reader, not a somewhat rude-sounding new school of thought. 'Go to Foz!' I tell the dog in the back. She nods into the rear-view mirror. We have gone through thick forests, the road undulating along the coast like the winding roads of the Scottish Borders, two Guardia bikers were following us for ages until they finally got bored and overtook.

Foz campsite found, first of all I park. I need a break. The *señora* surveys my German passport. There are lots of rose bushes flowering around and in front of the site. She hands the passport back over the bar, complimenting me on my rubbish Spanish. I like her. Then she tries to sell me some small property near here. Exhausted, I exit laughing, to find a space for the tent.

After some hearty cups of tea, I create a salad of two tomatoes mixed with some white beans from a jar, a tin of tuna and rosemary *schnipselled* (finely cut) over it. I spread a greedy layer of mayonnaise onto the bread. Topped with masses of black pepper, I decide that outdoor eating definitely rocks.

Checking out the toilets and showers later on has proved unrevealing but for an ancient, Victorian-looking, flat-bottomed glass decanter on a small round table. In it are three big, round heads of double-headed, old-fashioned, beautifully pink rose blossoms blooming their fantastic fragrance.

By 10.10 pm the grey light of the north is still not down. I am listening to the sounds of a Spanish three-year-old girl, saying the Lord's prayer, in Spanish, even her dad's deep sonorous voice, cannot invite her to sleep. Birds call out, the sea rushes backwards and forwards, in and out of the small sandy bay below.

26 May 2006

The first thing I see as I wake up is a tall yellow rose bush growing up a concrete wall. After tea, sardines and bread, Misty and I take the long walk along the beach into town. The day is getting hotter and hotter as I walk into Foz, looking for a tobacco shop. The no-smoking law operating in Spain since the beginning of the year has brought a few changes: now it is not possible to buy fags in a supermarket, though some still have machines as do many bars. There is no '*Estanco*' (tobacco shop) anywhere in sight. Funny how that word '*Estanco*' always makes me think of 'stink' which is of course exactly what burning cigarettes do. The butchers and butcherettes at the 'Dia%' *supermercado* keep calling everything '*Puta*' (whore) or '*Madre de puta*' (mother of a whore), then '*Hijo de puta*' (son of a whore or bitch). I wonder if they are having a swearing contest; their Spanish sounds different, more kind of squishy, perhaps almost like a Portuguese form of Spanish. I blow plastic money on some food, booze, shampoo and conditioner, and walk back along the high up coast with small sandy bays here and there. Brand-new houses are scattered all over the place.

Back at the campsite which is a converted military base, I think of Laurie and of war. In Spain, Franco or the Civil War are never mentioned, like Germans never mention Hitler or speak about 'the war' (World War II). The silent generation sits by, watching a new war; the war of affluence. Posh houses by the beach, ever faster cars, fatter people with fat children living on mass-produced junk. Like a great groaning fungus, money is spreading its blanket of haves and have-nots, rippling through the entire country. Though I have seen the least cranes in the north of Spain, the bug of money has bitten and is positively tangible, more houses on the beach, built from money earned in Madrid. The large houses are all empty, waiting for their summer visitors.

Down from the campsite, there is a vast deserted sandy bay. I fry in the sun for a while, watching the tide rolling in, and some rocks which will cut me off here for a time, sea gushing white-horsed surf against them. Dear Laurie, I have raced through your year in only one month, through a different-looking country. Seventy years after you were walking through a poor Spain, the country is now in the full grip of affluence. Tourism, consumerism, capitalism. Ouch, a stray bee has just stung my knee! Misty has found a stick and is leaping into the surf to retrieve it.

At the tent, lawnmower man moves up closer to the small palm tree on which my bikini is drying. Has every campsite got a nosy lawnmower man, moving in ever more closely, checking out new arrivals, I wonder, and quickly close the tent. I don't want its inside covered in cut grass.

'¡*No, mañana!*' the man calls out to me, cutting grass at

the patch next door. The guy must be all of seventeen. He is wearing what looks like a bee-keeper's helmet. The air smells of cut grass and gasoline stench as he starts up again, about six feet away, lustily mowing more meadow with his noisy strimmer. Exasperated, I grab my '*jamón ibérico*' sandwich, a tomato and some tangerines and head back to the beach, where the tide is ebbing and there is nothing but the play of a lazy wind, a rush of receding sea, a tired beach bearing imprints of barefoot humans, dogs, ants, a bee.

27 May 2006

Halfway through the night, I decide to change direction and not sleep with my feet higher than my head. The morning is grey and foggy. The Spanish in the tent near mine are still asleep; the numerous caravanners, mainly Dutch, are breakfasting. I feel like a prisoner in a military holiday camp ruled by Dutch men. The showers are pretty rubbish with only one hook, what for, soap-on-a-rope maybe. Oh dear, the mind is about to go off on its daily rant. I sling my clothes and towel over the partition, hoping they won't get soaked. Thin warm drizzle rinses the conditioner out of my hair. Today, I wear flares, a black sleeveless jumper under a black long-sleeved T-shirt with a wide neck, dark-pink tattoo-type patterns along one sleeve.

Having done the usual breakfast, I am going in the direction of Ribadeo, thinking sadly that I have missed the Playa de Las Catedrales and believing it must be hundreds of miles behind me. This morning, I feel that I am a hundred years behind myself. Fernando, I can't find the beach! Melancholia is trying to get a hold on my soul but I won't let it. On and on I follow the long, early morning road.

The car has just clocked up 2,000 miles when I see a sign for the 'cathedral' beach. Hurray! Fantastic! Here they are: six enormous, a hundred or more metres high stacks of rock - maybe slate - towering up from the bottom of the sea. It is low tide, and busloads of visitors are sprawling over the sandy sea floor, through rock pools, in and out of caves, cameras clicking here, voices going 'Ah' over there, digital video cameras whirring, people posing for photos, here an electronic flash, there a sudden dash as a freak wave soaks a rolled-up trouser leg.

The rocks are breathtaking, as if they should be under the sea, not sticking out from it. There is one huge archway towering above. Down here, I walk into dark caves with stripey, jagged and worn-smooth rock, water dripping down eerily from somewhere up high. This feels as if it has been touched by God's hand, lovingly moulding rocks and crevices.

But here is another coachload of tourists arriving, and Misty has just scared off the only bit of talent, about to cruise me. So it's back on the road.

I pass Aviles and Gijón, and turn right at Ribadesella to get me to Canga de Onis where I ask around a bit. Apparently Ribadesella goes mad in August, when a canoeing race takes place in the Río Sella with hundreds of canoes. OK, but I want to go to Covadonga. Some kind tourist information person gives me a map of the area, with campsites. I am told that they are probably closed until mid-June. Ah, not so good. From Covadonga, a serpentine road climbs up, up and round and up; don't look down now, just keep driving, to the lake, Lago Enol. There is a visitor centre here, and many people are wandering around the fabulous lake. We are in the National Park of the 'Picos de Europa' where some wolves and brown bears still survive, amongst the herds of mountain goats, wild boars, foxes, deer and more.

I go on to Lake Ercina, 1,108 metres above sea level, to find the refuge. A girl has got there before me and is talking in Spanish with the refuge keeper. He has a dangly wart under his left eye, and there is a button missing from his shirt, covering a bulging belly. The girl wants to know if a couple of girls and a bloke have stayed here. The man has seen no one. The girl is wearing a scallop shell around her neck. Her friends must be lost pilgrims. I ask her if she is German, just to be friendly. But she dismisses me with one look, saying, '*Ja, wieso?*' (Yes, what's it to you?) I ask the man if I can have a look at the '*dormitorio*' (sleeping quarters). One room has about a dozen mattressed bunk-beds crammed into it. Apart from the lovely log-cabin wood and a window, there is nothing else. One night's stay is eight euros. I don't fancy staying here with beady-eyed wart man. Something doesn't feel right. I reverse rapidly all along the rocky dirt track just to get away from the place. That girl wanted to steal my wind, that's it.

Back at the Lago Ercina, high up, surrounded by snow-capped mountains, Misty becomes a movie star. Some bored kids are throwing stones aimlessly into the lake, when Misty runs over, swims, then dives for the stones, again and again. Daddy gets his video going, they all love that diving dog. Misty shows off some more. I have just finished my luncheon tomato when I realize that I have lost the car key as well as the little purse containing all my plastic, my driving licence, a little cash. Holy smoke, what a shocker! I stagger back through the heat to the car praying for some miracle. I remember locking the car, but then what? The girl had definitely stolen my wind. My mind has gone blank. Will I have to ask at the visitor centre if anyone could break into my car please, and hotwire it so that I can get to…I don't know where to. I break into a panicky sweat, hobbling uphill, back to the car, my mind swooning. Everything could be lost at this point. I have no idea what to do. Well, dear reader, I can tell you, God lives. Here, in the boot lock, is the key with the little purse dangling from it, totally intact. Yes! God Lives! I feel like falling onto my shaking knees. Phew. That was a close one.

On my way down, I stop to listen to the church bells at Covadonga, 6 pm. Everybody else has to stop too. There are police officers whistling sharply, buses, cars, everybody stops. I have no idea what is going on and go to find a coffee in a small bar. It has T-shirts for sale with Celtic knot patterns, and others printed with the words *'Ser español es orgullo'* (to be Spanish is pride) *'Ser asturiano es un título'* (to be Asturian is a title). People buy trinkets and beer. It is very hot.

But what's this, now all the cars are moving again. Here is the cause of the delay. About a hundred or more runners have run steeply uphill to the chapel, and are about to run back again in the killer heat. They look exhausted, hypnotised and therefore slightly mad. I spot three women runners. A man stands at the roadside holding a hosepipe, spraying water over the sweating runners. Mayhem abounds. I have lost the dog's lead somewhere by the lake, and I am not going back up. We will have to use the posh one, made of white string with beads from a broken bracelet woven into it by Victor and Julietta.

Somewhere in the countryside, I am following camping signs and end up driving past an undertakers', directly into a dead-end path of neck-high nettles and a pile of sand. This is not a campsite. I don't know whether to laugh or cry. Reversing back out of it, the phone rings. Oh no, not now! Nettles are coming through the open window trying to brush my burnt face as I am looking over my shoulder, navigating the car. Then, looking at another dead campsite a bit later, there is a sudden invasion of a horde of teenagers on quad bikes, heading off into the wild forest for a bit of Saturday night fun. Further up the road are hordes of cyclists, all spandexed and shaded. At Avin I strike lucky. The site is open, but expensive. I ask if I can leave the car parked where it is and not pay for it, so that's a deal. However, it means that I have to carry the tent and my stuff, the sleeping bag, pillow, keyboard, duvet, drink, torch, lemon oil, car papers, passport, books, maps and the small plastic giraffe past all the other campers, neatly arranged in two small rows with a central path. People stare at me. There are two French gay couples, talent at least to look at, and English, German and Dutch caravans. Mist is settling as I put up the tent.

I am tied to a massive wobbly water bottle by the way

It is still very warm. I listen to cowbells singing like a little waterfall in a field across the fence. For dinner I have the last piece of rye bread and shiny slices of sweaty, tasteless, rubbery cheese with a tomato and tea. Something is trying to crawl under my bra and something else is up my bee-stung trouser leg. I grab the lemon oil. After dark and a few cheers inspections I remember Marilyn Monroe's line from a forgotten movie: 'It's so silent, you can hear your skin against your clothes'. Then I burst into a vibrant 'Amazing Grace', keyboard and all.

You would have thought that after thirty-four tunnels, I am now used to them, but no, not me. Every time I enter, terrified, and come out a gibbering wreck. And what about those viaducts that go on for miles, warning you of the wind, horizontal windsocks and all. Does gravity increase as you slow down? Part of some stretch along the E70 *autovía* today sounded like a shrieking Formula One car on racing tyres, the road screeching under the car so loudly, and me trying to find a crackly radio station to drown out the terrifying noise, going along at eighty miles per hour, the fag I have just put out having set fire to the other dead fags in the ashtray; now I have to deal with toxic fumes. And what are these coffin-sized houses on sticks all about? Are they dolmens? Is dead Grandad in there with lots of gaps in the walls for air?

During the night, it rains.

28 May 2006

I go a few miles up the road, park in a lay-by and put the tent over a fence by a waterfall to dry in the wind. I put the kettle on, have a few handfuls of miniature breadsticks and a tin of spicy tiny sardines, '*sardinillas*'. Driving on and on, the place feels like being in Austria: high craggy mountains, winding small roads, deep forests. The mist rising up over the mountains looks spectacular.

no i am here in the back

'You all right, Misty?' I ask the dog. Did she just think? Have I been on my own too long? Do I have a hairy mind-reader in the back? If the car starts talking to me, I'll have to turn myself in.

Here now, up in the blueing sky I spot five or six gigantic birds cruising one of the mountain tops reaching up to impossible heights. Through binoculars, I see the upturned wingtips...one of the raptors glides down closer, silently appearing like a flying carpet.

A bit further along, I find a campsite near Arenas de

Cabrales, twelve euros a night.

I set up camp and check out the toilets. The windows are decorated with owls and other forest birds in glass paint; a bath for babies, a tiny toilet (no paper) and a tiny low-level sink and mirror. Tasteful autumnal-coloured fake vine leaves adorn the walls, antique wooden pitchforks, lovingly varnished, are stuck to the walls between the toilet cubicles, we have ceramic toilet brush holders, good showers with three fat hooks, but what tops it all is the soothing music playing! From Schubert to Mahler to James Bond movie soundtracks, this is like an oasis for the music-starved (me).

I had bought some Asturian blue goat's cheese and some bread on my way here. Now, unwrapping the cheese in the heat, a dozen flies appear from nowhere. Fjochh! What a smell! Spread on the bread, it looks like blue pate. Misty gets the rind and sneezes a lot.

A graveyard up the hill behind the campsite is full of huge flat gravestones.

> Felix Prieto Anton
> 1887 - 1987
> El poeta de la vida (a poet of life)

This guy lived for a hundred years!

> Francisco Pereda Porrero
> Mi amor por Cabrales (my love for Cabrales)
> sigue vivo (I continue to live)

Or what about this one, no birthdate:

> Isabel Herrero Diaz
> (a little cross) el 17-8-1957
> RDO. DE HIJAS E HIJOS POLITICOS
> (remember the political daughters and sons)

I guess that Isabel must have been fighting in the Resistance during the Franco Regime and was probably murdered by his men. Her 'political' friends would have put up the anonymous gravestone.

I sing the Albert King song about the road going home to the graves and then set off further up the hill. Misty wants to chase a brown calf covered in flies. A blue condom wrapper lies on the rocky path. I hear a cuckoo. There are black redstarts, buzzards, a fat kestrel, hoopoes, later, an owl. Too hot to walk on; yes, Laurie, what a wimp I am. I check out the campsite bar. Over a beer, I ask the guy if he has any camping gas '*cartuchos*'.

'Sure, but I will have to open the shop,' he says, going off for a key. A TV blares cars racing loudly around some track. The guy's girlfriend is reading a magazine, oblivious to the din of the TV above her, her cigarette, forgotten in the ashtray, smoking itself. Opening the shop means going into a room next door. Soon I have my *cartucho*. Outside, I have another beer and watch the swallows nesting under the roof of the bar. A small cloud is sailing by, making the mountaintop temporarily invisible. I have found out that beans and maize are dried and stored in the houses on sticks or stone legs. No ladders for mice! Aha!

Uphill, behind the tent, is a row of wooden chalets for hire. They all have names. '*Aguila*' is the golden eagle, '*Ardillo*' the squirrel, '*Jabalí* ' the wild boar, and '*El Zorro*' the fox. All very tasteful. Dinner tonight is a cooked treat from a tin of Asturian bean stew with a big lump of pure white fat and three pieces of chorizo.

I spend the first part of the evening doing a bit of people watching and even get new neighbours. She has the kitchen set up in minutes, consisting of a table with everything on it, a neat pile of chaos. They are young and happy people. Across from me is a fat mama sitting inside a caravan, blatantly staring at me through her open door. I have fallen in love with a tree trunk but I am too lazy to draw a picture of it. Staring at the tree maybe confused the staring woman. I can't stand it any longer and go off to the musacked toilets. Like the guys in the showers this morning, man, only one toilet and sort of shared showers, going '*je t'aime*' and sighing. I gave them a wonderful Joss Stone song and left. All I've got is imperfect foot nail varnish, a face covered in old stains and holes, shiny with lemon oil, nicotined teeth, and bleached eyebrows.

'Where are my eyebrows?' I rant at the mirror. The eyeliner has melted in my bag, and I am saving the lipstick for unforeseen events or emergencies. It was the tick in my hair this morning that really did it. I nearly had a heart attack. I would rather drive through another tunnel than have a tick attached to me! Thirty-seven or thirty-eight tunnels by now? I am beginning to lose count. Bad sign.

On the way back to the tent, the three new tent blokes check me out on their way to the showers. I wish they wouldn't. My self-esteem is at rock bottom. I should go to the wee bar and talk with people, maybe ask the barman to demonstrate the cider pouring tradition, but I don't have the nerve. My mind is shouting at me, 'You need to get a life! You need to get a love life!' I ignore the uncalled-for advice and, instead, I return to the tent to spend the rest of the evening squishing small insects and encouraging spiders to leave. Maybe by now they are throwing cider over their heads into horizontally held glasses in the bar. It is the done thing in Asturias, a skill to show off or get very wet. In 2002, there were 3,146 people who all did it at the same time!

The cicadas are moving closer, chirping away. Something in me feels fed up with camping. A snail has chewed two holes in the mosquito net. What a nerve. I am glad when Mr Whyte and Mr Mackay turn up. I tell them how I am getting sick of mountains and crave for the sea. I think there is sea in my blood. Between us, we make up this little song:

>'I'm gonna leave you in the morning
>I'm gonna pack up my tent
>I'll leave you all still yawning
>as I break up the elasticated sticks
>and release the stretches and clicks
>of the 100% Nylon heaven-sent
>cloth enclosed space
>never leaving a trace.'

Oh dear.

Away from the night-time opening and closing of plastic caravan doors sounding like walk-in, industrial fridges, far, far away, wolves are listening quietly, knowing they are 'protected'.

29 May 2006

What a night!

The football pitch lights stayed on shining bright neon till midnight. But even the music in the toilets went down after that. The couple next door stopped flirting, just as the eight climbers returned from the pub and started farting. After a restless sleep - so warm - the dawn chorus abruptly stopped, and I heard the quietly whispering first drops of rain. I fell asleep again and into a pseudo-nightmare - the tortoise was back with a long purple crustacean streak all along my right cheek.

I rarely close the outer door of the tent and wake up with rain merrily dripping onto my feet. Propelled into sudden action, I jump up, rescue what is still dry into the car and go for a shower. The water takes ages to get warm. I even wash the dog's lead with washing-up liquid when the new conditioner bottle falls off the wall into the other cubicle. I have to retrieve it starkers, ducking and diving, hoping no one comes in at this ungodly hour. After a short, sharp breakfast, I stuff the wet tent into the back and leave. The guy who runs this place is obviously some mountaineering medallist; there are plaques, cups and photos of climbers all over the walls of his office. It reminds me a bit of bundles of butch birdwatchers, ornithologically hunting for bluethroats or pelicans, crawling through mud on their knees and elbows, binoculars focused on some rare species. Like yesterday, I dry the tent in a lay-by, somewhere near Panes.

Should I go to the cheese-making museum, or do the cider trail, or both, or neither? A huge snail is sliding off a fence post. Some people eat them, sucking them straight from the shell, still alive. A dark-blue aquilegia is flowering by the turquoise waters of the Río Cares. Misty is mad because she cannot find a way down to it. At long last, the sun is trying to break through the clouds. A car even goes by, and the tent is nearly dry. In Panes, I find out from the '*ayuntamiento*' (town hall) that the cave of La Loja is closed until June. I buy some cider from a dark shop smelling smokily of '*jamón*'. Up and round many more roads, I end up high on top of some other mountain shrouded in clouds, to visit a grand cave, El Soplao, full of crystals and Mother Nature's treasures. Thirty euros to get in. I cannot afford that. You go into the cave on a small train. Just looking at the pictures almost gives me an attack of claustrophobia. By next year, there will be a huge visitor centre here. There are piles of bricks, cement mixers, and men already busy, smoking and talking.

I feel grey and grumpy. I have had enough of the entire area and go back down the grey mountain, along grey asphalt roads under grey sky. To the sea! As I am driving along, I am wondering if life in the mountains drives people here crazy. They dress up in high-heeled clogs, with three heels under each shoe, donning red and black jackets and skirts, shiny buttons, lacy scarves, and then they start dancing in small circles, after pouring cider over their heads. I guess, it keeps the wolves off. Some wolves are kept in cages around here, as well as brown bears. The last thing I need this grey morning is to look at a caged-in wild animal.

I zip on to San Vicente, find the campsite and set up camp here, for three nights. I need a break. You are right, dear reader. I was a bit low this morning, maybe because the days of the journey which I have counted so often, and the money, are now down to single numbers.

Suddenly, the sun bursts through the sky. Hurray! I have a cup of tea and Philadelphia on crunchy bread, waiting for someone to book me into the campsite. Energised, I dry the stinking damp duvet on the car roof, put up the washing line and settle myself in. The heat is rising, the surf looks fantastic. I'm off for a swim. Lazing around on the beach for the afternoon, I recount the order of the historic events I had been musing over for so long.

First, there were the caves of the Old Stone Age, although history goes back even further as the oldest pieces of human bone in the whole of Europe prove. They have been found near Burgos. Then came the Ice Age, followed by people probably migrating from northern Africa. At around this time, the '*dolmens*' (tombstones) were built. Would it be the Iron Age next when, eventually, copper was discovered? Naturally, metal revolutionised farming techniques as well as warfare. After this, Phoenician and Greek people migrated into Spain. They brought new skills with them such as writing and making music on instruments. They introduced money, olive trees, farm animals like chickens and donkeys, and wine. These 'Iberians' had dark skin and hair. Then, when the Celts moved in, bold, blond, drinking beer and eating lard, the party really started until the Romans and Visigoths arrived, all bringing more skills, languages and religious beliefs. Which is when the Muslims came into the country. They lasted until 1492. Aha, Isabel and Fernando are at the wheel, and Columbus is about to sail off into the distance. Marco Polo however had travelled to Asia two hundred years before. Seeing communications in those days were very slow; ideas and experiences were slow to spread. But they did.

Cervantes and El Greco, a hundred years after Columbus, were also 'ideas' people; Cervantes invented a novel style of writing whilst El Greco started experimenting with perspective and painting long, drawn-out figures. The Renaissance had begun sometime in the fourteenth century in Italy. Its school of thought was based on humanist ideas, the revival of interest in Classical Antiquity, naturalism and a fidelity to nature. El Greco (the Greek) was originally from Crete but had learnt to paint in Rome before coming to Spain. So he had brought the technique of perspective with him. Cervantes was just a total rebel in my eyes, sick of 'the status quo' and bored to death with the false ideals described as 'chivalry', he thought up his ironic response and wrote 'Don Quixote'. However, there was one more person, living in Italy at the same time, who also had ideas, theories and experiences. This man was Galileo Galilei, astronomer and physicist. He not only discovered the constancy of the pendulum's swing which was later applied to the regulation of clocks but he also proved the law of 'uniform acceleration of falling bodies'. He described craters on the moon, stars of the Milky Way, Jupiter's satellites and the phases of Venus.

But his acceptance of the Copernican system was rejected by the Catholic Church. He was threatened with torture from the Inquisition and had to publicly renounce his 'heretical' ways. I am convinced it was Galileo who said, '*und sie, die Erde, bewegt sich doch*' (and yet she, the earth, does move).

Back to Columbus having proved that the world was round, I wonder what happened. Did he have to keep this secret, silenced by the Catholic Church who were happy enough though to accept gold and silver by the shipload? Just a hundred years later, Galileo totally knew not only that the world was round, but indeed, that it moved! And he was right, but not allowed to go public with his proof. My mind is boiling with rage at the maltreated heroes. What would have happened if they had had better communications and all got together to pool their data, I ask myself. Maybe they would just all have been burnt at the stake together. By the way, it was just another hundred years until the birth of Samuel Hahnemann, the father of homeopathy, a revolutionary discovery in the world of medical treatments.

Laurie Lee was also a revolutionary man, returning to Spain in 1937, walking over the Pyrenees in December, to fight with the Resistance. I admire these heroes who stuck to their convictions and took action despite facing opposition and possibly death.

Starving, I return to the tent, my head swirling with thoughts of rebellious heroes. Still plateless, I am dining on another tin of '*fabada asturiana*' with extra beans which have been festering or maturing more since before Santiago and fat slices of the found *chorizo*, eating directly from the saucepan/kettle. Over half a packet of mixed nuts with buckets of tea, I watch three bikers arrive on softly purring Harleys. The couple set up a tent. Could this group of people be some of the original fans of 'Zen and the Art of Motorcycle Maintenance', I wonder vaguely. Why do I not have the nerve to go up and talk to them? The single guy cleans his bike, wiping, polishing and posing in leather. Though tempted, I decide it is probably best not to go over to ask him for a ride. It would seem a bit off my style. Yet after two thousand miles in a hot car, the prospect of gliding along, freewheeling on the back of a motorbike is pretty attractive. But one does not want to appear desperate.

I have a fag on the beach watching the surfers' acrobatics, and the terns catching fish.

At this time of year, terns fly around in a figure of eight with a little silver fish in their beaks, looking to attract females for breeding. Translated into words, their body language seems to say, 'Yo, have fish, come fly with me, I'll bring more fish for you.' How elegant are these 'sea swallows', how piercing their lonely shrieks.

30 May 2006

I am in Altamira's big replica cave. Yes, yes, I've had breakfast. The real cave is now closed to the public because of fears that the increasing humidity caused by us humans breathing will destroy the precious paintings. It dates from 12,000BC. Wow! The replica cave is real enough for me. There are lots of railings, thank God, because I feel like falling over every time I look up at the curved cave ceiling. Drawings of bisons are set into the rocky, lumpy ceiling. One stone has the perfect hump of a bison's back. Ochre, red and charcoal-black is painted into carefully scratched outlines. Here are some of a bear's paws. Tiny hands - the people were pretty small at 1.20 metres average height - are put upon the rock, and then, almost like graffiti, red paint is blown through a pipe or straw. Lift the hand off and, hey presto, caveman was here! I understand the Spanish guide fluently. The whole place is almost magical. There are bones and antlers, carved, sharpened and pierced, all over the place. Suddenly, three life-sized figures, how do they do that, with laser beams or what, appear in a corner, a woman, a boy and Grandad. Cracking nuts, the boy eats whilst

Mum empties a leather satchel of berries, leaves and fruits she has collected. Grandad blows the fire back into life. It all looks so real! Here is Dad coming into the cave, carrying fish on a stick, his harpoon made from bone. Surveying the ceiling more, gripping the banister, I see the red *'claviformes'*. They definitely look like spaceships. Maybe the whole scene of the *'claviformes'* is depicting an entire spaceship war? Side-on, one of them looks like the traditional flying saucer. I am aghast. All these paintings are depicting what was really scary for cave people: big bisons and huge bears, and spaceships? The guide says that human hands were painted on the walls to say, kind of, 'small me human, I was here'.

In the big exhibition hall, TV screens show how to knock a roundish stone just so, so that it splits off a sharp knife-blade shape. This then gets knocked lightly with a small wooden hammer, looking like those Irish ones, I forget the name, shaping and sharpening it. Now it is perfect for de-barking sticks to make arrows and Ikea-type furniture - the leather strings and sticks for the frame and seating of a chair. I love it.

The three HH (Hamburg number plate) leathered-up blond bikers do not respond to my '*Hummel, Hummel*!' in the true Hamburg way. The guys should respond '*Mors, Mors*!' honouring the tradition of calling the water carrier with his wooden yoke, a pail of water suspended from each side; making fun of him as if he were a bee or '*Hummel*' in *platt-deutsch* (flat-German), legs laden with pollen. He in return, fed up with the weight of it all and constantly getting teased, would call back boldly, '*Mors! Mors*!'(Arse! Arse!) Ah well, can't say I didn't try.

Back at the car, I don't believe it. The dog has been playing the keyboard; there are unmistakeable muddy footprints all over it. She has even switched it on!

i was dead bored the batteries must have wobbled out of place because it did not make a sound

I stock up on Spanish food and whisky to take back to Scotland, talk of 'taking coals to Newcastle', in a supermarket, bending the plastic more. Getting lost on the way back to San Vicente, I go past what looks like a nuclear plant and a cement factory, belching toxic smoke. Oh, Laurie, this is awful! After a late luncheon, almost an entire loaf of bread, Philadelphia and '*jamón*', in the shade of a car park, I consider my case:

I have now done forty-two tunnels and over two and a half thousand miles of Spanish roads. Not everybody can say that when asked, 'What did you do in May 2006?'

The other half of the bag of nuts is for dinner with lovely thick brown tea.

31 May 2006

The morning sees me in San Vicente de la Barquera, a small touristy place by a gorgeous bay. I have found the Iglesia de Santa María de los Angeles and want to see what is said to be 'the best piece of Renaissance funerary art in Spain', just to find out what 'funerary' is. I buy a postcard of the funerary statue of the inquisitor Antonio del Corro, reclining and reading after asking someone when the church is open. The reply is quick. 'Never', I am told. 'Maybe at 5 pm when there is Mass.' I'll be on the beach by then.

In a vegetable shop in town, I mistakenly ask for two kilos of beers (*cerveza*), when I meant to say '*cerezas*' (cherries). I am met with a very odd look. Nobody laughs but me. Oh, dear, can't win them all.

I take the dog for a walk along the grassy slopes looking like Northumberland coastline, high above sandy beaches. A farmer is moving his beautiful Friesian heifers to another pasture along the single-track road. There are only a few houses on the spring-flowered cliff tops. The sounds of singing and piano playing emerge from one place, a BMW parked outside, as if Sabina himself is in the house, making his sad rhythms of soulful, Spanish passion.

We turn back to walk into the setting sun. A farmer has fired up his fabulously ancient tractor and sings full-blast above the noise of the roaring engine, an aria of uncaring happiness. What a voice! I am jealous.

Oh no, Misty has rolled in something dreadful. She has turned bright yellow. It is time for another swim. After all, she has to visit the vet tomorrow to get her passport stamped, before getting onto the boat. I too take to the sea, feeling like a swimmer baptised.

Any food today is completely unremembered, but Mr Whyte and Mr Mackay help me celebrate my last night in Spain, the end of the journey.

1 June 2006

I am on the boat. This is the first time I have ever managed to grab a chair on deck. Bob Dylan is singing in my head 'I was riding on the Mayflower when I thought I'd spied some land...' breaking off into hysterical laughter and starting to sing again, as I am scanning the horizon. I tried on some perfume in the duty-free and now smell like a grapefruit. Waiting to pay for a postcard of the 'Pont Aven', a man told me that the ferry was hit by a forty-foot wave last week, one metre of water in the cabins, portholes smashed, the bow damaged. Everyone was herded upstairs wearing life jackets! He went on that 'It is best to have a bottle of Scotch inside you in these events, and after the second one, you don't really care, do you.'

The prices in the restaurant are extortionate at twelve euros for a starter, so I have a piece of bread with some boiled pig's head, a cup of tea, there is free hot water here, and a tomato. Guess dinner will be much the same. The dog is in the kennels. There is a man who watches the dogs in the kennels on video. He sits in a wee cubicle and watches the dogs. He tells me the oddest story of a woman climbing into a large kennel to spend the night there, her hand stretching through the bars in the morning reaching out for coffee and some bread brought by her companion. Well.

It took me ages to find my cheapy, inside cabin, no fear of smashed portholes here. I dumped my filthy rucksack on the floor. Then I saw the crisp white linen of my bed. I have so looked forward to sleeping in a real bed!

Watching the sunset, I am hearing Laurie's words in my head, how he had stood on deck 'watching Almuñecar grow small and Spain folding itself away....I saw again, as I lost them, the great gold plains, the arid and mystical distances, where the sun rose up like a butcher each morning and left curtains of blood each night', when my nostalgia is interrupted by a voice calling my name. Am I imagining this?

Before me stands Rob! Hurray! We've both made it! He missed the boat last week because he decided to cycle up to Covadonga and the Picos. Cycled!

I immediately call upon Mr Whyte and Mr Mackay to help us celebrate.

We spend the night on deck, aim-spitting cherry stones into an empty glass.

The last word

Back in Edinburgh the following evening, the words of Sean Connery come into my mind: 'I feel like I've done fifteen rounds with Mike Tyson, but I feel I've won'. I am celebrating my arrival with my family and uncountable bottles of Spanish wine, when at 1.30 am there is a policewoman at the door saying my car has been smashed up. The car's papers show an address in the Borders. How do the police know that I am in my daughter's flat in Edinburgh?

Dear reader, if you know the answer, please let me know.

P.S. I have one thing to say to you Misty Blue.

oh yeah what is that then

You are the best dog in the world.